TEACH ME

TO

Pray

TEACH ME
TO
Pray

LEARNING TO
PRAY LIKE JESUS

D. Qwynn Gross

DESTINY IMAGE® PUBLISHERS, INC.

P.O. Box 310, Shippensburg, PA 17257-0310

"Speaking to the Purposes of God for This Generation and for the Generations to Come."

This book and all other Destiny Image, Revival Press, MercyPlace, Fresh Bread, Destiny Image Fiction, and Treasure House books are available at Christian bookstores and distributors worldwide.

For a U.S. bookstore nearest you, call 1-800-722-6774.
For more information on foreign distributors, call 717-532-3040.

Or reach us on the Internet: www.destinyimage.com.

ISBN 10: 0-7684-3108-5
ISBN 13: 978-0-7684-3108-7

Abbreviated version of this book previously published under ISBN: 879-1-60702-236-7
Library of Congress Control Number: 2008933197

For Worldwide Distribution, Printed in the U.S.A.

1 2 3 4 5 6 7 8 9 10 11 / 13 12 11 10 09

DEDICATION

Father,
I dedicate this book to You.
Thank You for the opportunity to serve in this manner. It is my
privilege to offer what You have given. May You be glorified
in the lives of every reader, and may You show Yourself faithful in
the lives of every doer. I ask You to confirm my word as Your servant
and perform my counsel as Your messenger (see Isa. 44:26).
May every word tug at the heart of Your children. I appreciate
Your loving-kindness toward me as You have given me the
opportunity to do something I only dreamed about.
I praise You, for You have blessed me indeed.
Thank You, Lord.

ACKNOWLEDGMENTS

Special thanks to my husband,
Trevón D. Gross, Sr.
for his encouragement to pursue vision;
to my children,
Trevón, Dianna, and Sarah,
for their patience;
and, to my parents,
Dwight P. and Birdie W. Midgette,
for their support in my spiritual growth.

Bishop I.V. and Lady Bridget Hilliard
"I've got the grace to do this."
Thank you.

TABLE OF CONTENTS

FOREWORD

I am often asked to write forewords for members, partners, associates, and friends; however, due to time constraints and the sheer volume of requests, I regretfully decline most. My heart and passion for prayer caused me to reconsider Pastor Qwynn Gross' request to read and write the foreword for *Teach Me to Pray.*

It is with godly pride that I write the foreword for one whom I consider a true spiritual daughter in the faith, Pastor Qwynn Gross.

It is by faith that we receive the promises of God, but we must open our mouths to speak the will of God into our lives. Today, there are millions of people living outside of the will of God for their lives because they have no revelation on prayer. This book will impact, inspire, and equip you with wisdom on prayer that will lead you to God's purpose for your life.

Most people have the desire to pray yet do not follow through for many reasons. Some do not understand the power of prayer. Others do not have revelation on how to pray. And still, others may say, "I just don't have the time to pray."

TEACH ME TO PRAY

Pastor Gross' book will remove every excuse, hindrance, or obstacle you have to obtaining a powerful prayer life. Her book provides an anointed and purposeful pattern for prayer that will awaken your spirit and desire for intimacy with God through prayer.

It is through her submission that she is able to share her testimony of an effective prayer life and teach it to us with such simplicity. Pastor Gross' well-written blueprint for a better prayer life will keep you immersed until the very end. After completing the book, you will be eager and excited to apply the principles to your own prayer life.

You will also learn how she continued to pray and stand in faith until arriving at a place of victory. When you look at her today, you see the glory of God showcased to an unbelieving world. This is due to her unwavering and unconditional commitment to prayer.

I have had the pleasure to watch Pastor Gross's life, and as I read this book it brought to my remembrance the zeal in my heart when I learned the power of prayer. Once you have the revelation, it is always your desire to get the message to others who may still struggle in an area that you have overcome. This testimonial book on prayer may be the missing and very essential element necessary for you to know that you can ask, believe, confess, and receive.

You are about to be blessed as you begin reading her commitment to pray. I pray that the Spirit of God will cause her message to encourage you, and that this book gets into the right hands at the right time to transform a generation into a praying generation. Get ready to be completely engrossed as you begin your journey to a wonderful and purposeful life through consistent prayer.

Lady Bridget Hilliard
Wife of Bishop I.V. Hilliard and
First Lady of New Light Christian Center Church
Houston, Texas

INTRODUCTION

I suppose having a father in my home made it easier for me to appreciate the relationship God desired to have with me as my heavenly Father. I grew up in a home with both parents. Though my father was typically gone due to work, time at the pool hall, or time in front of the television, I knew he loved me. As I look back on his ways, I see a family that existed by grace. The family dynamic wasn't perfect; it was simple. My dad said very few words, and usually when he spoke it was with passive authority. A simple suggestion was enough to carry out the directive.

Though I wasn't threatened by my father with spankings, I can honestly remember one threat; and that was to learn to spell my name. After a couple of hours of his drilling, D-i-o-n-n-e M-i-d-g-e-t-t-e, he finally left the room with one statement: "You better know how to spell that name when I get back." Needless to say, I learned to spell and write that name. I never forgot.

Though my dad was quiet, I always respected his voice and loved being around him. If he let me go with him anywhere, the ride was always quiet but nice. When he spoke, it was enough to move closer to hear. When he laughed, I was amazed. When he affirmed, it warmed my heart for a lifetime. To me there was an unspoken love I could count on. My response would be to honor my dad as much as I could even as a grown woman.

My mother was always vocal, truthful, and consistent. To me she could always take care of herself. She always had something to say, though she considered herself quiet. Her influence on my life was as profound as my father's. She threatened and swiftly carried out the threat. She was always quick to point out cause and effect. Her message was stern though she regularly embraced and showed affection.

With this combination, I grew up seeing and learning an over-arching message: Disciplined living leads to reward, and consistency produces a decent living. I didn't resist the message. I was compliant and prepared to replicate what these two people presented as normal.

From my experience in their home, I grew to be very disciplined in my approach to life. For this reason, accepting Christ wasn't difficult, and surrendering to God wasn't strange. God in supreme authority was in a position to receive the best of what I had to offer Him: me. Moreover, His authority and my surrender to His authority meant I was willing to yield to His way, His plans, and His purposes.

Before my commitment to God, my relationship with Him was nonexistent. God was a distant Being who was relevant only at death. I didn't know a mortal could actually interact with *God*. I honestly didn't think that God cared about us to that extent. After one mission trip, however, I had a revelation that this God was living and that this God was worth every effort to get to know. My empty title of being a Christian now had meaning. Hence, I would honor Him as much, if not more, as I honored my natural father—with compliance and without resistance.

To comply would mean directions were necessary. To get directions, I studied my Bible regularly. As I read the Word of God, I realized talking to and hearing from God was not just possible but normal. And God desired it.

Studying God's Word also helped me discover what God's will was for various situations. Motivation to pray came when I positioned myself to join others who prayed regularly. I was a college student at the time and heard about a group of ladies who gathered to pray. Without much thought, I asked one of the ladies if she would pick me up so I too could pray. She welcomed me and was diligent in letting me know when they were praying. Though this "time to pray" was much more than I anticipated, it would be the hinge that kept me faithful to God.

During this time of prayer, I learned to apply to prayer the discipline I already practiced as a lifestyle. I had an expectation of what a disciplined life would bring me, and I applied that expectation to my diligence in seeking His face. My expectations were met as God continued to teach me how to pray, giving me a greater understanding of what prayer is from His perspective.

Maybe you're one who wants a greater understanding of prayer and a more effective prayer life. Reading my experience may spark a desire for more in your prayer life, but understanding what Jesus taught regarding prayer will, I pray, launch you on a journey in prayer that is akin to nothing else in life.

TEACH ME TO PRAY

Undoubtedly, the disciples observed that Jesus purposefully spent time alone in prayer with the Father, and they knew that Jesus had the answer to all things. So they asked Him to teach them how to pray. Being Jesus, He was willing and able to give answers. Matthew 6:9-13 records Jesus' teaching on how to pray:

> *In this manner, therefore, pray:*
> *Our Father in heaven,*
> *Hallowed be Your name.*
> *Your kingdom come.*
> *Your will be done*
> *On earth as it is in heaven.*
> *Give us this day our daily bread.*
> *And forgive us our debts,*
> *As we forgive our debtors.*
> *And do not lead us into temptation,*
> *But deliver us from the evil one.*
> *For Yours is the kingdom and the power*
> *and the glory forever. Amen.*

In Mark 14:37, Jesus chided a couple of disciples saying, *"Could you not watch [pray] one hour?"* First Thessalonians 5:17 reads, *"Pray without ceasing."* I think we can conclude one thing: we are expected to pray. Jesus' response in Matthew 6:9-13 addresses the issue of how to pray effectively. However, if we pray these words verbatim, our prayer will last from between twenty-two to thirty seconds max. What, then, is Jesus talking about? How can I pray all the time and for at least one hour with meaning?

I believe we can pray the words of Jesus just as He said—beyond oration and memory but completely in line with His will. Further, I believe we can look at the words of Christ and see a pattern that we can use to build a prayer life that's continuous and effective.

16

Introduction

Father,
Thank You for teaching me how to pray so that I
know You and please You.
Thank You for having a plan for my life and for
giving me a future and a hope. To fellowship with
You is my extreme honor and privilege.
You are forever my God.

CHAPTER 1

THE TRUTH
ABOUT PRAYER

Prayer is something that we're all familiar with. Though we all have different expectations as to the outcome, most of us have decided to talk to the invisible God at one time or another in our lives. Our ability to communicate is not the problem. We all know how to voice our concerns, express our heartaches, complain about our problems, or show a level of piety, but we don't always know if we can expect an answer or if we were heard in the first place. As a result, our prayers span from the quick and perfunctory to the intentional and focused. Our uncertainty regarding prayer minimizes our desire to pray regularly or with purpose and sincerity, unless we are prodded by unwanted situations in life.

When we cry out, "O, God! Help me, Lord!" or "Jesus!" we acknowledge Him as greater, bigger, and stronger. That's commendable, but there is more to prayer than that. Our initial cry to God is the place where interaction with Him should begin. Just as calling someone's name would get his or her attention for a conversation, so our call to God gets His attention for further dialogue. And, just as relationships are developed with people, God is available to everyone for an individual building of relationship. Our pursuit of Him measures and determines the intensity of that relationship. And while there are times we feel our conversations with God are insignificant to Him, we should always be reminded that our willingness to call on God is truly His desire. James 4:8 says, *"Draw near to God and He will draw near to you."* No matter how minor or major your issue, God welcomes you.

Prayer and Relationship

Many of us say we believe in prayer, but we engage in it like it's the lottery: If your number comes up, you're a winner; you get an answer. If your number doesn't come up, bong—try again next time. This mentality is not God's plan for your life. Psalm 91:15 says to believers, *"He shall call upon Me, and I will answer him..."* There is no ambiguity; there's no gamble, just a definite promise. When you call, He answers.

Then there are those of us who don't mind calling on God, but our sincerity is conditional. It's akin to a street person asking for ten dollars and promising to pay it back: he or she will bless you if you give the ten dollars and curse you out if you don't. That sounds harsh, but we do the same thing with God when we start with prayer and revert to luck or an eight hundred number when we're not sure we received our answer. Matthew 15:8 says, *"These people draw near to Me with their mouth, and honor Me with their lips, but their heart is far from Me."*

Now most of us would never compare our prayers to the lottery, nor would we want our sincerity questioned, but our approach to prayer reveals what we believe. If we want to uphold integrity toward God, we must always approach Him knowing prayer is completely about relationship. That's why Christ came to give His life, for us to appreciate and enjoy relationship with God. When we honor our relationship with God, our love for Him will grow, our trust in Him will heighten, and we'll never question His opinion of us or His true desire for us.

Every biblical account of those doing right in the eyes of the Lord shows that the immortal, invisible, all-wise God is interested in relationship. In each encounter, their stories show examples of a God who intervened for them, fought for them, had compassion upon them, spoke to them, and was available to them. From Abraham who believed God and was counted as righteous, to Moses who didn't know God until His introduction at the burning bush, to King David who unashamedly served God with a loyal heart and willing mind, these and many others experienced the hand of God because of a relationship. Not every relationship was perfect, but in each case God showed Himself as very present, very interested, and very protective of His own.

From their testimonies written in Scripture and my own relationship with the Almighty, I know prayer works 100 percent of the time. *"But if from there you seek the Lord your God, you will find Him if you look for Him with all your heart and with all your soul"* (Deut. 4: 29 NIV). It's a promise. He makes this promise again in Jeremiah 29:12-13: *"Then you will call upon Me and go and pray to Me, and I will listen to you. And you will seek Me and find Me, when you search for Me with all your heart."* And again in Psalm 145:18, *"The Lord is near to all who call upon Him, to all who call upon Him in truth."* There will always be a response to our seeking God when we call on Him with all of our heart and when we call on Him in truth. Truth is His Word (see John 17:17). *"Now this is the confidence that we have in Him, that if we ask anything according to His will, He hears us. And if we know that He hears us, whatever we ask, we know that we have the petitions that we have asked of Him"* (1 John 5:14-15). Too often when we pray we expect our answer to come like the countdown of a microwave oven. Give it a few seconds, beep, ready. What we should realize is that God's answer may not be seen, but it's definitely in our possession at the time we pray using God's Word. When Jesus cursed the fig tree, the tree was dead after He spoke. It started dying from the roots, though, for a time, the leaves still showed signs of life. By morning the process was complete. This tree didn't die when the disciples noticed dry leaves; the tree died when Jesus spoke (see Mark 11:13-14;20-22). My point is, you may not *see* your answer to prayer the moment you pray, but you must *believe* that you receive your answer when you pray and then you will have it (see Mark 11:24).

In addition, the answer may not come as you expect, but you must remain encouraged that God hears you because He cares about you. When the crippled man looked at Peter and John at the gate called Beautiful, he thought they would give him money, but he got something greater—his healing (see Acts 3:1-10).

I recall being a youngster and calling on the name of the Lord. My mother had just spanked me, and I lifted my tearful eyes to God and said, "If You exist, will You help me?" The earth didn't shake; I didn't see a glow in the room, nor did the events of the evening change. Yet, with confidence, I can say that the prayer I said as a pre-teen was answered. Years later, I recognized His intervention as I traced my steps from that moment until college when the Gospel was presented in a way that I could comprehend and truly accept.

From my vantage point there was no detectable change the day I prayed, but a shift began as God aligned people, events, and occasions for the good of me and my family.

Remember, the steps of the righteous are ordered of the Lord (see Ps. 37:23). When you call on Him, you may not understand the perceived delay, but He begins to put people and information in your path that lead to your answer. Answers to prayer are not always as they seem, but there will always be an answer if you continue to believe. Always.

Let me also add, I know God speaks to the obedient for the sake of the lost, confused, and needy. Jesus Christ is the best example of that: *"For to us a child is born, to us a son is given, and the government will be on His shoulders. And He will be called Wonderful Counselor, Mighty God, Everlasting Father, Prince of Peace"* (Isa. 9:6 NIV). The Savior was anticipated, but they were not looking for a child. *"For the Son of Man came to seek and to save what was lost"* (Luke 19:10 NIV). Yet, as a child He came and fulfilled prophecy to the letter. Here's another example. When Israel cried out for deliverance from Egyptian bondage, God went to talk to Moses but deliverance wasn't immediate; it took time for God to prepare Moses to be His answer to Israel's prayers. Israel cried out during the oppression of Midian, and God went to Gideon. It took time to prepare him too. Once these two men were ready to obey God, they were part of God's answer to the cry of Israel.

I recall going to England with my husband on a business trip. I wasn't as excited as I should have been to go, but I went reminding myself how much I always wanted to see this part of the world. Upon arrival, I decided to get my nails done. I heard the Lord tell me to let the nail tech know how much He loved her. In obedience I shared the love of God. She told me she just asked God that morning if He truly cared about her and if He loved her. Never question if God has your answer! While she was praying, God was sending me to her—from the East Coast of the United States! I tell you, God positioned me to tell her the good news; I came with her answer. Her call to God and my obedience gave her the answer she needed when she cried out to God. Suppose I had decided last minute not to go on that trip, or not to share what I heard God say to me? God would still have answered her, but there may have been a greater delay in preparing the next person willing to obey and go to her.

I am only one of many. I remember hearing Kenneth Copeland, a well-known evangelist, talk about how God had him travel to some distant land. He didn't have a scheduled meeting there, and he had no other reason to be there except that God told him to go. In obedience, he prepared his plane and traveled to the other side of the world just to share the Gospel of Jesus Christ to one woman. Kenneth Copeland normally speaks to crowds of thousands, yet he traveled a great distance for the sake of one person. God didn't care about how much it cost him to travel; He gave him the resources to go and the instructions to go for His cause.

I am convinced God answers prayers, including yours. Your answer may not yet be seen, but it doesn't mean your prayers are neglected. Just because you don't see something happening doesn't mean there aren't credible reasons for the delay (see Gen. 25:21), divine interruptions taking place (see Dan. 10:1-14), and/or various preparations necessary (see 1 Sam. 1; 2:11-21; 2:26-3:1-21). We don't always see what it takes to make a champion out of somebody, but once he or she has arrived, we all recognize it. Rarely is there an empty reason for what happens in life. As parents, we frequently tell our children things they don't understand, yet their lack of understanding doesn't speak to our being negligent. My son, for instance, didn't understand why I banned his use of the kitchen, but I recognized that he wasn't ready, as food was being cooked unattended. He didn't understand why he couldn't make a quick egg sandwich, but as a parent, I was clear it was for the good of all of us. When he's ready to return to the kitchen, I'm confident he'll be more responsible.

The Essence of Prayer

"Seek Him while He may be found; call on Him while He is near" (Isa. 55:6 NIV). Prayer is the opportunity every person has to interact with God. I call it an opportunity because whenever we call, He's available to us; He can be found. We shouldn't take it for granted, however. In Amos' day, God said He would send a famine—not of food or water—but of *"hearing the words of the Lord"* (Amos 8:11). Never would we want to be without the voice or leading of God. There would be no point to prayer if He didn't speak. Where would we be if He were silent, unwilling to talk to us? We're at His mercy; that's why we should seek Him with a grateful heart.

Prayer is a time when we can talk to God about our concerns and surrender to His purposes for our lives. When we communicate with others, we're taking time to appreciate and respect them for who they are. When we communicate with God, we're taking time to acknowledge and accept His supreme authority. Prayer affords us the opportunity to express appreciation to God through worship and adoration. In prayer we also receive direction from God, gain greater understanding, and obtain peace as a result of the promise. To ignore prayer is to ignore solutions to every quandary in life. It's the same as having money in the bank and not accessing it during a critical need. You can ignore it, but it doesn't make sense.

Prayer is so rich. To truly fellowship with God Almighty is a pleasure we should all take the time to pursue. If we would recognize that our approach to God often determines our ability to receive, we would shift from skepticism to hope and from pessimism to expectancy. Our communication with God is designed to build relationship beyond requests for this, that, and the other. Psalm 103:7 records that God made known His ways to Moses and His acts to Israel. While Moses interacted with God in obedience and built a relationship with Him, Israel cried out for needs alone.

Matthew 21:21-23 says, *"I tell you the truth, if you have faith and do not doubt, not only can you do what was done to the fig tree, but also you can say to this mountain, 'Go, throw yourself into the sea,' and it will be done. If you believe, you will receive whatever you ask for in prayer"* (NIV). Notice Jesus says, *"If you believe, you will receive whatever you ask for."* You cannot receive in prayer what you are unwilling to believe. So while some consider their good deeds as a way to get God to answer them, the Bible doesn't talk about titles, charities, and works as a way to get God to answer prayer. It does say we have to believe; according to John 6:29, believing is the work: *"This is the work of God, that you believe in Him whom He sent."* Like any work, there are benefits. Hebrews 11:6 says, *"But without faith it is impossible to please Him, for he who comes to God must believe that He is, and that He is a rewarder of those who diligently seek Him."* Not only will we receive our requests when we pray, but we are rewarded for being diligent in seeking and tenacious in believing. Glory to God!

How Should I Pray?

There is a way to effectively talk to God. I've seen people stand, walk, look around, or kneel with folded hands during prayer. I've heard people yell their prayers (guilty!), and I've seen people praying without making a sound. Personally, I bow before Him during private devotion and pace back and forth during intercessory prayer. At this point, I'm convinced that the positions used to pray are not as significant as the actual words being said.

Eyes open or eyes closed? *"Watch and pray"* found in Matthew 26:41 (NIV) justifies eyes open while tradition encourages eyes closed. We can defend standing up while praying using the Scripture, *"And when you stand praying"* (Mark 11:25 NIV). Even yelling can be substantiated as Ezekiel used a loud voice (see Ezek. 11:13 NIV), and Jesus cried out loudly (see Matt. 27:46,50 NIV); additionally, the Israelites called on the Lord with loud voices on many occasions. Hannah, in contrast, prayed silently; her mouth moved, but no sound was heard (see 1 Sam. 1:13 NIV). From these observations, I think it's safe to say that the physical practices of prayer mean very little. God is not interested in our outward appearance and displays; He's more interested in the heart (see 1 Sam. 16:7). The exterior should conform to what is in the heart. So our humility, respect, and love for God are seen by how we comport our lives, not by how we choose to pose in prayer. Understand, there will be a day when every knee will bow before Him (see Rom. 14:11; Phil. 2:10), but our daily fellowship with God can consist of one or all of these positions of prayer.

You choose your position, your style, your volume, but how you communicate with God will make the difference in your results.

Have you ever continued talking to someone without realizing that he or she had left the room or that the phone call had abruptly ended? It can be frustrating because everything said was in vain. I want to know that when I talk to God that I am adequately communicating. Have you ever made valid points concerning an issue and someone else dismissed you and your comments? Whether in worship, with supplication, with petitions, or thanksgiving, I not only want Him to hear me, but I want to have confidence that He places value on what I'm saying.

If you're a parent, you should know what I mean. While our children are precious, sometimes they say things that are not necessarily, in and of themselves, of great priority to us as parents. Nevertheless, we listen because we value our children enough to listen and bring correction, encouragement, or laughter where needed. Our Father is the same. What we have to say may not be high on the list of priorities as God looks at the state of the world; but God cares about what we care about. We are important to Him, and He values what we say even if correction, confirmation, or encouragement is needed. Philippians 4:6-7 says, *"Be anxious for nothing, but in everything by prayer and supplication, with thanksgiving, let your requests be made known to God; and the peace of God, which surpasses all understanding, will guard your hearts and minds through Christ Jesus."* We never have to wonder with God; He's always interested in the cry of our heart.

Praying the Word

Praying the Word is important. God does hear the prayer of our heart. For the sake of results, however, it is important to find our heartfelt concern in the Word of God so our expectation can be set based on biblical promise, not whim. Our ability to align our concerns with Scripture forms the basis for our confidence in receiving what we need. If He didn't want us to have it, we wouldn't see it in Scripture, but if we find it in Scripture, we know He is not withholding it from us (whatever "it" is to you). God hears all of us, but we must recognize that He acknowledges His Word foremost (see Isa. 55:10-11). So why not use the Scriptures, literally and comparatively, to direct how we interact with Him? Our peers and people we respect have given us many models of how to pray, but the best models to follow are the scriptural ones. For example, *"Elijah was a man just like us. He prayed earnestly that it would not rain, and it did not rain on the land for three and a half years"* (James 5:17 NIV). He was heard, and his prayers were answered. I'd say he's an example to follow. Even better, Jesus taught His disciples how to pray. And we can glean from that. If we look to Scripture for an illustration of how we should pray, we have an opportunity to see the problem and the solutions used. We can follow or set aside these examples after seeing the end results; however, if we only follow the models of today, we may miss God at pivotal moments in life.

I remember when a man was asked to pray in a large assembly. He stood gripping the microphone, and after a long and very awkward delay, he blurted out, "Thanks, amen." The crowd mused as the program continued, but that was the day I promised myself to pray with a point and pray with meaning. That man made an indelible impression in my mind and the message still reverberates within me: never stand in front of people to pray if you have nothing to say!

On another occasion, I remember visiting a church's intercessory prayer meeting. I anticipated a great meeting because the attendance was strong. What I was surprised to find was senior leadership and members praying for their pastor using the same words repeatedly. From one person to the next they all tried desperately to say words beyond, "Bless him, Lord" "Just bless him" "Help him" and, "Help him, Lord." They obviously wanted to say more as they painstakingly paused between each "Bless him, Lord," only to resume with anguish as they reiterated the same variation of words. Virtually everyone in the room took a stab at praying for him. After many rounds, it was clear there was no one able to pray for the pastor in a way that spoke either to specific needs this pastor may have been facing or to the general issues every pastor would want prayer for. Their intentions were honorable; otherwise, they would not have been there, but the execution came terribly short of what I suspect was really in their hearts. They were sincerely stuck.

Thankfully, we don't have to be stuck in prayer. The Bible speaks enough about God's will for us to use even if we pray the very words we read. After witnessing that, the message to me was to give thanks for the time I spent reading and studying His Word. *"Write* [the Word] *on the tablet of your heart"* (Prov. 3:3).

Then I've heard, on more than one occasion, others pray in a church service with more than a hundred parishioners in the room as they prayed for themselves, their children, and their lives. They never once included the congregation that had their heads bowed in agreement with them, nor did they reference the pastor, the church, or the leadership. Prayer for them meant "prayer for me." *"I* want to thank You; *I* need You; Bless *me,* Lord; Bless *my* child, Lord." *Me, myself,* and *I* were all we heard. Bewildered, I started thinking about how selfish the prayer sounded. Shouldn't that prayer be said during personal time with God, not with the church? *I, I, I, I!* I thought they were supposed to pray for everyone when in a public arena! The message I gleaned from that experience was that there is a place and a prayer for every occasion. From private time with our Father in the prayer closet (see Matt. 6:6) or in a public forum (see 2 Chron. 6:12), we must fashion our prayers for the occasion.

And finally, I've experienced one or two people who prayed a dissertation while everyone patiently waited to begin Thanksgiving dinner. It's time to eat, not filibuster!

My point is, there is a moment for every kind of prayer. There is a time to pray for self and a time to pray or intercede for someone else. There is a time to request and a time to just give thanks. There is also a time in prayer when praise, adoration, and worship are offered. And then there are times of inquiry because we lack understanding. Most of the time, we should use God's Word alone to pray, but there are times when our prayers are from the overflow of our heart. Then there are times to pray with reverence—in silence. And the greatest part about our silence is it's during this time that we'll actually hear God speak!

I bring these examples up because our culture presents prayer as uncomfortable and difficult, but it doesn't have to be. Unfortunately, too many of us simply don't know what to say or where to begin, so prayer is ignored or repeated verbatim night after night and in any forum. Maybe you've graduated from the poetic, "Now I lay me down to sleep" prayers, but you're still unsure of how to articulate the matters within your heart. You know what you want, but you can't necessarily say the words that pinpoint the exact issue. I have good news! I referenced it earlier, but I really want you to understand how to pray effectively. Praying is easy when you use the resource God has given, literally. The Word of God is the source that guides us in our relationship with our Father. The Bible tells us who God is in character and what His desire is for our lives. Thus, we can pray with knowledge. I cannot perform a job without a job description, and I can't perform optimally if I never learn what my boss appreciates and what is an aggravation to him or her. Likewise, if we're willing to study the Bible, we'll gain understanding from the parables, principles, and precepts given for application in our prayer lives. With an understanding of who God is, we are better equipped to communicate with expectation.

In the second section of this book, you'll find the prayer Jesus taught the disciples to use, known as the "Lord's Prayer." I have sectioned off each stanza to give you a pattern that will benefit you during prayer. You'll find this biblical resource useful as you see how applicable it is in developing a relationship as well as making petitions and interceding for others. With a systematic and daily regimen of the "Lord's Prayer," you'll be well on your way to a successful and efficient prayer life.

It's perfectly okay to use the resources made available to us to express our issues and desires before God. The Bible offers the greatest tried and proven methods for building a relationship with God; in the process, we also learn and appreciate what relationship means to God.

CHAPTER 2

A STRONG
RELATIONSHIP

For any genuinely strong relationship, communication is necessary. In the natural, we develop long-lasting relationships through the amount of time and attention that we give to each other. From a casual acquaintance to a true friend and companion, we categorize who and what a person is in our lives. How many times have you heard a couple say they knew their spouse was their mate the day they met? That willingness to pursue the building process with an expected end is the same willingness we must use toward God. For too many of us, God is a casual acquaintance rather than a true friend because time and effort have been minimally invested in the pursuit of His friendship. I can't neglect communication with my husband, my family, or friends if I want a strong relationship, nor can I neglect or randomly approach God if I want a strong relationship with Him.

Like any natural relationship, it's always evolving, and though God doesn't change, we do. We'll either grow closer to Him or more distant. The more I talk to certain people in my life, the stronger my relationship will be even though we mature and change over time. God does not change, but our constant communication with Him enables us to evolve into people who uphold the title of Christianity with true godly character. Have you ever noticed that the more you communicate with a person, the more you imitate him or her? Maybe you never used the word *like* in a sentence more than two times, but since you've made friends with a neighbor who uses the word constantly, you now say *like* five times in a sentence just as the neighbor does. I use to work with an older woman who wore dentures. Consequently, she always needed to use her thumb to push her front teeth up. In every conversation, day after day, for more than a year, I watched her secure her teeth with her thumb. Then one day, out of the blue, I was talking and pushed up on my very real front teeth! I knew immediately why I was doing that. I had been around her too long.

Constant communication makes for a strong relationship because when I know my God, I begin to emulate Him in character (love, patience, kindness, faithfulness). Communication also yields a higher regard for the other. When I'm talking to a friend and I hear a need expressed during casual conversation, I recognize that need and work toward meeting it if I'm able. God is always able. So our time with Him offers us favor to receive from Him. Psalm 34:10 says, *"But those who seek the Lord shall not lack any good thing."* This is a promise given to seekers of the Lord.

Like you, I have something in mind when I'm communicating with others. Either I enjoy their company, genuinely want to know them better, have a question, have a comment, or I have a request. I should have something in mind when I talk to God, too. When I talk to God, I'm looking for results. For me, those results are a stronger relationship with Him, answers from Him, direction for assignments given by Him, or something very concrete. If you honestly assess your prayer life and find it to be arbitrary, tentative, strained, and filled with doubt and unbelief, it may mean you need your Bible to be your guide as you pray. Using your Bible will help you appreciate who God is and discover the good that He purposes for you. Growing in the knowledge of Him not only builds your confidence in seeking but will also prepare your heart with expectation, and build your relationship for sweet communion.

If the Bible overwhelms you because you just don't know where to begin, I would say start praying from the Book of Psalms to give honor to God and from the words of Christ in the Book of John for submission to God. As you read, highlight Scripture that you could use to pray. Over time your highlights will be the guide you need to pray effectively. As I mentioned earlier, in the second section of this book you'll find a pattern that you may use to apply the Lord's Prayer in your life too.

CHAPTER 3

THE TEMPLATE OF HIS WORD

Communication requires effort; it means we inquire for the sake of greater understanding and then apply what we've learned. When we study God's Word we are learning His ways and understanding His desire. For instance, if you want a relationship with God, you'll find First John 2:23 says, *"Whoever denies the Son does not have the Father either; he who acknowledges the Son has the Father also."* That information lets us know where relationship with God can begin—through His Son, Jesus Christ. If you want to know how to love God, John 14:21 says, *"Whoever has My commands and obeys them, he is the one who loves Me. He who loves Me will be loved by My Father, and I too will love him and show Myself to him"* (NIV). You see, the information we need to interact with God effectively is found in His Word, the Bible.

It becomes indispensable then to have a Bible and to use it. Primarily because God places a premium on His Word. He says, *"Heaven and earth will pass away, but My words will never pass away"* (Matt. 24:35 NIV). John 6:63 says, *"The Spirit gives life; the flesh counts for nothing. The words I have spoken to you are spirit and they are life"* (NIV). And in Matthew 4:4, Jesus quotes the Word (see Deut. 8:3) as He makes a point about its preeminence: *"It is written: 'Man does not live on bread alone, but on every word that comes from the mouth of God'"* (NIV). These are just three Scriptures that show us how powerful and necessary the Word of God is. The Word of God won't pass away; it gives life, and it is how we are to live. Thus, using the Word of God to pray is the solution for effective communication with God.

I mentioned earlier that you could just pray from your heart, but from this kind of prayer you cannot expect results 100 percent of the time. From this kind of prayer you're pulling on God's mercy to move toward you. It does work. Israel groaned and cried out to God because of the oppression of Egypt (see Exod. 2:23). Then God looked and was concerned for them. The CEV says, "He felt sorry for them" (Exod. 2:25). And their answer came. The ideal situation, however, is that you pray His promise, He hears His Word and will not allow it to return void (see Isa. 55:11), and then He answers. This can be your reality 100 percent of the time if you'll pray His Word with your heart and believe. We can guarantee results by praying His Word concerning situations that are beyond us. His Word has an answer to everything we'll ever face in life. If we use God's Word to pray, we'll see how well it speaks to the matters of our heart. In addition, when we're in God's Word, our time with Him will be that much sweeter because we're reminded of who God is and can give thanks with understanding and sincere gratitude. Prayer is rewarding if we know how to communicate effectively.

When I pray using God's Word, two things happen. One, I'm speaking life. Everything God created started with His Word, "Let there be" (see Gen. 1:3). Then, John 1:1 tells us "In the beginning was the Word...." When you and I use the Word to pray, we are praying life into every situation, circumstance, and care around us. If you want something to turn around for you, begin with His Word! God's Word is not empty; it makes the difference. And two, when I pray the Word, I'm speaking His will. *"...If we ask anything according to His will, He hears us. And if we know that He hears us, whatever we ask, we know that we have the petitions that we have asked of Him"* (1 John 5:14-15). When I pray the Word, I am praying God's will! Without the Word, you may begin praying cliché's that you thought were biblical, what you heard someone else say, or what you think is right. With the Word, you'll not just be accurate, but you'll be able to set your faith. Now you may be wondering if you're expected to memorize the Bible. You don't need to deliberately memorize every Scripture, but you do need to read the Word, study the Word, and identify the relevance of the Word to your life. Then when you're ready to pray, Holy Spirit will remind you of the Word you've read or studied and you'll pray fluidly and with strength. (*"But the Helper, the Holy Spirit, whom the Father will send in My name, He will teach you all things, and bring to your remembrance all things that I said to you"* John 14:26).

So I encourage you to have your Bible with you during private time with God. Pray what you're reading. Pray for yourself, for your family, for your church, for whomever the Scripture best applies. Not all Scripture appears to be a prayer, but you can make it a prayer by slightly modifying the words or by capturing the essence of what you're reading for personal application.

For example, if I were praying for the pastor as referenced earlier, I can look at Colossians 1:9 and pray verbatim, "Lord, fill Pastor _____ *'with the knowledge of* [Your] *will in all wisdom and spiritual understanding; that* [he] *may walk worthy of* [You], *fully pleasing* [to You], *being fruitful in every good work and increasing in the knowledge of* [You].'" Or, Ephesians 1:17, "Father, give Pastor _____ *'the spirit of wisdom and revelation in the knowledge of* [You].'" Or, Father, I thank you that *"no grave trouble will overtake"* Pastor _____ (Proverbs 12:21). Or just, "Father, thank you for a Pastor who loves you with all of his heart and with all of his soul and with all of his strength" (see Ps. 107:8, Deut. 6:5). Any pastor would want these kinds of prayers! You're not just praying according to the will of God, but you're praying with life! When you pray the Word, your expectation will change because you'll appreciate the written word as God's promise to us as believers. Hence you can set yourself to believe God, knowing He honors His Word.

Eventually, you won't need to use the Bible every time you pray because His Word will be written on the tablet of your heart. And the Holy Spirit will continue to draw out of you what is needed for yourself and anyone or anything else you want to pray for.

What I am giving you is the answer to a strong prayer life; though it requires personal effort, your fortitude will yield great returns. It doesn't happen overnight, but it does happen before you know it. Studying and learning God's Word will make you keenly aware of what God thinks about you and the situations around you.

Learning the Word for prayer is no different than going to flight school and learning slang for greater efficiency in communicating. For the pilot, the objective is to communicate the maximum amount of information using a minimum amount of words. You could keep talking the way you always do, but you'd lose a lot of time. Similarly, if I became a truck driver, I would have to learn expressions that are not used in everyday conversation, but among truck drivers they are concise, clear, and common—"10-4?" If you're after results, check how you're communicating. Are you whining or complaining? Are you waiting for a response after you've talked? Are you doubting God will or can before you even ask? These are questions we should answer. If the answer is yes to any one of those questions, reevaluating your approach to communicating with God is necessary.

When you take time to learn God's Word, you'll find what is *written expresses very much the care of your heart, for "There is nothing new under the sun"* (Ecc. 1:9).

What is even more profound is that we serve a God who tells us *"I love those who love me, and those who seek me diligently will find me"* (Prov. 8:17). For He is not far from any of us (see Acts 17:27).

CHAPTER 4

SPIRITUAL LIFELINE

A lifeline is a very thick rope also known as "an anchored line thrown as a support to someone falling or drowning. It's a line shot to a ship in distress. It's a line used to raise and lower deep-sea divers."[1] When rescuers send divers down to the ocean floor, the divers could be miles away from the anchored ship. The divers are equipped with a lifeline so that they are not just safe, but they are assured that if they need to be pulled out of any situation, they only need to tug on the lifeline, and those in authority will pull the divers to safety. If for some reason the divers are without a lifeline, there may not be a rescue, and the divers could be lost at sea.

Prayer is a spiritual lifeline. It is the one thing that can rescue you from any situation in life. No matter how deep the situation, no matter how ominous it appears, no matter who you are, you can tug on what I call your lifeline. You can talk to God, and He who has all authority can and will pull you to safety. The Israelites were not perfect people, but they knew where to turn when in trouble. They weren't really obedient people; they were disloyal and showed remorse only when trouble showed up. Their obstinacy was an affront to God, yet He always responded when they used their lifeline. You may need a rescue at every turn in life, but you can be assured that God doesn't want you lost. He will come to your rescue if you'll use your lifeline.

The lifeline is used in space too. As astronauts explore the galaxy, they have a lifeline attached so they don't float away. Maybe you started with the Lord, and you began to explore the options available in the world. You can be encouraged: You won't drift away lost forever if you use your lifeline. God has equipped you with a lifeline so that when you call on Him, He is available to rescue you from any and every threat. All you need to do is pull on your lifeline. When you open your mouth to talk sincerely to God, you have begun pulling. Get your heart right before God through repentance and call on Him for deliverance. His promise in Psalm 91:15 is sure, *"He shall call upon Me, and I will answer him; I will be with him in trouble, I will deliver him and honor him."* You may not be able to figure out how to get out of the mess you're in, but there is a God who delivers by many or by few (see 1 Sam. 14:6 NIV).

I would like to offer a disclaimer. The Christian life is not designed to be a life filled with problem after problem after problem. If you are experiencing an entourage of problems and it's a lifestyle (i.e., can't pay mortgage, can't keep utilities on, borrowing from everyone known and unknown, can't keep a job), there may be a larger issue in play. Perhaps you are in a season of testing, but perhaps the issue is a matter of organization, discipline—or even plain rebellion. I define rebellion as knowing what is right to do and refusing to do it. It's not just sin, but it is considered witchcraft: *"For rebellion is as the sin of witchcraft, and stubbornness is as iniquity and idolatry"* (1 Sam. 15:23). In any case, it's important to take a brutally honest assessment of your life and ask the tough questions. If there is rebellion in your life, you can open the door for God to help you by acknowledging your sin: *"If we say that we have no sin, we deceive ourselves, and the truth is not in us. If we confess our sins, He is faithful and just to forgive us our sins and to cleanse us from all unrighteousness. If we say that we have not sinned, we make Him a liar, and His word is not in us"* (1 John 1:8-10). That is why it is important to sincerely repent (change our behavior)—so we see results from our prayers.

There are times when we will be tested, and those tests are challenging. But a test comes to prove who we are and what we really believe from the heart. The function of a test will be addressed further in a later chapter.

Tugging on Your Line

Recognizing that you have a spiritual lifeline should bring relief, primarily because *"whoever calls on the name of the Lord shall be saved"* (Rom. 10:13). What a blessing! You don't need to be perfect; you don't need to bottle everything in; you don't have to stress yourself into sickness and disease. God is available to you. However, knowing *how* to tug is just as important as knowing that you *can* tug.

Of course tugging is crying out to God, but if we want to tug hard, we must use our faith. As Christians, there are times when we call on God and receive a complete miracle. Then there are times when we call on Him and He gives us the wisdom we need to fix the problem. There are also occasions when we must exercise our faith toward the problem. Unfortunately we've understood faith to be a static position. We don't do anything with it; we just pronounce we have it. Then in tough situations we encourage ourselves or others by saying, "You just have to believe." Scripturally, however, we see that faith isn't a state of being, neither should it be static. Our faith is to be used, and our goal is to grow in faith or build faith. The way to build or grow it is found in Romans 10:17 which reads, *"Faith comes by hearing, and hearing by the word of God."* Though God gives each of us a measure of faith (see Rom. 12:3), too often we use that measure for salvation alone. Anything beyond salvation and we're unsure how to get God to move on our behalf. We simply don't have the faith to muster a change. For this reason, it's important for us to intentionally hear the Word of God so our faith can come in greater measure and our prayers yield results.

Our goal should always be to build our faith on what God has said, in general and for specific concerns. Doctors tell us what they think. Bankers advise. Teachers give information. Lawyers counsel. And in each of these settings we believe what they have to say. The more we hear their report on a subject, the more convinced we are that their word is truth—except their word isn't truth. Their word is fact. God's Word is truth! John 17:17 says, *"Sanctify them by Your truth. Your Word is truth."* Then, Psalm 91:4 says, *"His truth shall be your shield and buckler."* In other words, God's truth is our armor and our protection. His Word protects us from the unwanted facts that invade our lives. Yet if we don't use His Word, it cannot protect us, nor can we grow faith regarding it.

Psalm 145:18-20 says, *"The Lord is near to all who call upon Him, to all who call upon Him in truth. He will fulfill the desire of those who fear Him; He also will hear their cry and save them. The Lord preserves all who love Him...."* So when we pray, we are admonished to remain in truth, God's Word. We cannot change our opinion because the facts contradict God's Word. Growing faith is using faith. And when we use our faith, we're pulling our spiritual lifeline!

I remember moving heavy furniture on my own one day and feeling a shift in my lower back. I ignored the strain and continued my day trying to stretch the uncomfortable feeling away. I stretched throughout the day but by day's end it was a nagging, dull pain. I decided to call on God for help. I passively declared Isaiah 53:5, *"by His stripes I was healed"* and continued with my evening routine. By night I was still in pain, and the choice to go to the emergency room or to pursue my lifeline with greater urgency became very necessary. I chose to pull on my lifeline! I went in my prayer space to seek my Father. Using His Word, I called on my Father that night using His Word with the conviction that His Word must work. I used my faith and when I left that room I was assured by Him I was healed. The pain was still there but I had a surety this time. I went to bed; and somewhere in the middle of a very deep sleep God fixed my back, as I awoke to a quick jerk and a loud *crack*. It startled me at first but with thanksgiving I went back to sleep. I didn't need to get up and check my back because I knew God healed me when I left my prayer room. Now the work was manifested. I rose the next morning completely restored! I tell you, our God is a shield and a buckler if we'll hold fast to what He says. If we continue in His Word, His Word will be the lifeline that saves us from every trouble or care.

The decision I made to use my lifeline is the same decision we must make regarding anything and everything in life. The lifeline is the Word of God and if we'll pull, or at times, yank by believing [using our faith toward] what He promised, He will always reel us into safety.

How you decide to use your faith will determine how hard your tugging is. My decision to pursue God beyond a passive quote of

Scripture, and my disregard of a doctor's help, was my decision to walk by faith. Everyone gets a chance to make their own decision on how to use their lifeline. If you ignore the principles of faith, there is no tug on the lifeline. If you're casual with your faith, the tug on your lifeline will be feather-like; hence, your results in prayer will be barely detectable. If you decide to strengthen your faith, you'll find your tug to be strong enough to yield results in greater measure. Like a muscle, the more I use it, the stronger it is and the more I can lift. If I don't use the muscle, it will atrophy. Similarly, if I use God's Word to confess truth in the midst of pain, difficulty, and uncertainty, my faith will strengthen and my resolve will become unyielding.

Faith, then, is more than important; it's a priority for every believer who wants to pray and make a difference. Again, faith is an action word just like pulling a rope is a verb. It's not just a state of being; it's something we're doing. We're either walking by faith or by sight. As believers, *we walk by faith, not by sight* (2 Cor. 5:7)! We've got to operate our faith by speaking what God promises for our lives. This is tugging and it is akin to what Paul in First Timothy 6:12 calls *fight*[ing] *the good fight of faith* (NIV). The fight is declaring God's promise when life contradicts what you read in your Bible. When you persistently pray God's Word in the midst of unwelcomed facts, you have started playing tug of war. For example the Word says, *"When a man's ways please the Lord, He makes even his enemies to be at peace with him"* (Prov. 16:7). The Word is truth, but every day you face an antagonist at work. Listen, your confession in praying God's Word is the only thing that will cause you to prevail. The facts may seem overwhelming and they may even grip you, but when you speak God's Word over the circumstance, the situation must yield to the name of Christ (*"My enemy must be at peace with me"* (see Prov. 16:7)). My Bishop, Dr. I.V. Hilliard, always says, "My situation cannot change the Word of God, but the Word of God can change my situation." That's real! Change your situation by using the Word! Use your faith by confessing His promise and you'll see His promise override anything you're facing, including the "enemy" at work.

When you pray His Word and confess truth throughout the day, you are tugging on the lifeline and combining faith with your prayers. Faith is so important. Jesus went to His hometown in Matthew 13:58, but Scripture says, *"Now He did not do many mighty works there because of their unbelief."* Hebrews 4:2 says, *"For indeed the gospel was preached to us as well as to them; but the word which they heard did not profit them, not being mixed with faith in those who heard it."* Faith must be applied to the Word of God that we know. When we mix our faith by using it, we're tugging on a lifeline that truly does make a difference.

Exercising Faith in the Midst of Fear

No matter how far away you may be or how difficult your problem, when you pray God's Word, you're building your faith and you're tugging on your spiritual lifeline. God's response is to pull you closer to Him, closer to the manifested promise, and further away from the problem. You may say, I don't know a lot of Scriptures. Consider Romans 10:13: *"Everyone who calls on the name of the Lord will be saved"* (NIV). And starting now, "Lord help!" will suffice.

The lifeline doesn't mean you have all of the answers; it means you have the one Answer who encompasses everything you need, God. Let's look at King Jehoshaphat in Second Chronicles 20:1-3. He wasn't a perfect king; he was a king who knew he had a lifeline:

> *It happened after this that the people of Moab with the*
> *people of Ammon, and others with them besides the*

Ammonites, came to battle against Jehoshaphat. Then some came and told Jehoshaphat, saying, "A great multitude is coming against you from beyond the sea, from Syria; and they are in Hazazon Tamar" (which is En Gedi). And Jehoshaphat feared, and set himself to seek the Lord, and proclaimed a fast throughout all Judah (2 Chronicles 20:1-3).

The first thing we can note is that as a king who was supposed to be in control, Jehoshaphat honestly looked at the situation and recognized it was above him. The Bible said he was afraid, and if we put ourselves in his shoes, I think we can understand his fear based on the multitude coming against him. His response to fear was to turn to the Lord. This king's response is the same that we should have when fear grips our hearts and controls our minds. *"I sought the Lord, and He answered me; He delivered me from all my fears"* (Ps. 34:4 NIV).

Like Jehoshaphat, we need to seek God and pull on the lifeline. Jehoshaphat tugged on his lifeline much harder as he added fasting to his praying and began to speak of God's strength and power: *"O Lord God of our fathers, are You not God in heaven, and do You not rule over all the kingdoms of the nations, and in Your hand is there not power and might, so that no one is able to withstand You?"* (2 Chron. 20:6). He then reminded God of the covenant He made with Abraham: *"Are You not our God, who drove out the inhabitants of this land before Your people Israel, and gave it to the descendants of Abraham Your friend forever?"* (2 Chron. 20:7). Jehoshaphat humbled himself before God, saying, *"O our God, will You not judge them? For we have no power against this great multitude that is coming against us; nor do we know what to do, but our eyes are upon You"* (2 Chron. 20:12). King Jehoshaphat is praying! He's tugging on his spiritual lifeline.

When you pull on the lifeline, you recognize you have no power. You are at the mercy of the one pulling the rope back to the ship, if you will. Jehoshaphat didn't for one moment use his status as a reason to hold onto pride. He recognized they were in dire straits unless the Lord came to their rescue. He didn't have the written Word for reference, but He had an experience in the God who had helped him and his people in past. He tugged his line, and God started reeling him and the people to safety. That's what happens in prayer. Communication. It's not one-sided; you speak, and God answers. God speaks, and you respond. Communication is the ability to speak from the heart and hear with humility. In other words, he deferred his authority to the One in supreme authority.

God responded to Jehoshaphat's call through a prophet Jahaziel:

> *"'Do not be afraid nor dismayed because of this great multitude, for the battle is not yours, but God's.... You will not need to fight in this battle. Position yourselves, stand still and see the salvation of the Lord, who is with you, O Judah and Jerusalem!' Do not fear or be dismayed; tomorrow go out against them, for the Lord is with you"* (2 Chron. 20:15,17).

At this point, he had a number of options: He could have rejected the entire word, he could have accepted only parts of the word, or he could have taken the entire word as his plan for victory. Jehoshaphat listened to the whole counsel of God. You, too, get to choose. God gives directions when He answers the cry of His children. Our decision to obey is our decision to win or lose. Jehoshaphat chose to receive the entire word by being obedient to it. He began to position himself through worship and praise because He expected God to do all that He promised.

Expect From God

In addition to praying with knowledge of God's will and His Word, we must pray with expectation. Expectation in prayer is a priority. Remember, the purpose of prayer is not simply to have a reputation of being a person who prays, but to have results when we pray. If we're only interested in being known as those who can pray, then we'll be empty and look like the church in Revelations 3:1-3: *"...I know your works, that you have a name that you are alive, but you are dead"* (Rev. 3:1). The title of being a prayer warrior can be true, or it can be a façade. The outside looks authentic, but it's a sham. It's like going to a play where the stage props look real, but it's only a front. Why pray if there are no results?

One of the greatest expectations we should have is that our prayers are interactive with God. Interaction requires at least two parties, and in prayer those parties are exclusively you and God. Sure, you can invite others to join you, but then we're talking about corporate prayer or intercessory prayer. For now we're talking about you and God. When we use God's Word to pray, He not only gets our attention (on His Word), but we get His. And this is what we all want, God's attention. When Hezekiah cried out to God after hearing the prophet pronounce his death sentence, he prevailed upon the principles of God. He said, *"Remember, O Lord, how I have walked before you faithfully and with wholehearted devotion and have done what is good in your eyes"* (2 Kings 20:3 NIV). He was getting God's attention by reminding Him who he was. Then he fell into a fit of tears. Hezekiah prayed not knowing the outcome but expecting God to uphold integrity and honor him as a loyal, not perfect, servant. By verse four, the prophet is told to go back and tell Hezekiah, *"I have heard your prayer and seen your tears; I will heal you"* (2 Kings 20:4-5 NIV). I tell you, get God's attention not just with tears but through His Word!

The story is told of a Gentile in Matthew 15:21-28 whose daughter was *"severely demon-possessed."* She came to Jesus expecting to be helped and began to communicate with the Son of God. Dismissing offense, she focused on what she came for. In the end, Jesus calls her expectation and determination *"great faith."* That *"great faith"* is what each of us should have when we go to God, expectation and determination.

What do we expect? We expect God to uphold His Word! If we don't know what His Word is or what His character is like, we'll adopt the world's view: a God who gives and takes; a God who is unpredictable and impulsive; a God who only executes judgment; a God who cannot be trusted. With this mindset, how can anyone pray with confidence or pray with expectation? Study the Bible, go to church, and know God as He is. He reveals Himself through His Word, and through His Word you will learn what you can expect from Him.

As believers, we're striving for an unbending, unyielding determination to receive what is promised in His Word, undaunted by how things appear and convinced God is the answer. He wants us to be strong not weak, certain not tentative, loyal not fickle, bold not timid! For example, if an official came to you and told you that your name was Susie P. Susie, you would reject that information out of hand. If she insisted that was your name and she was about to change your birth records, you would fight without apology and with confidence; you wouldn't change your opinion nor would you yield to the official's assertion. God wants His children to have that resolve when promises are found in His Word. We are not moved because we know our God! He'll do everything He's said because He's not a man that He would lie (see Num. 23:19 NIV). We must be thoroughly convinced of His Word if we're going to pray with expectation. When I read, *"A faithful man will abound with blessing"* in Proverbs 28:20, I set my heart to receive those blessings by being faithful in every area possible. I don't expect humankind to recognize me, but I'm expecting God to see and reward me just as He promised. I don't compare myself to another Christian because I don't know how faithful they are beyond what I can see, but when blessings come my way, I receive with thanksgiving, knowing God has honored His Word in my life. My expectation extends beyond another person's experience and drives me toward my own testimony.

Psalm 5:2-3 reads, *"Listen to my cry for help, my King and my God, for to You I pray. In the morning, O Lord, You hear my voice; in the morning I lay my requests before You and wait in expectation"* (NIV). Pray the Word and expect from God!

Herein lies our confidence. Jesus said in John 16:23-24, *"And in that day you will ask Me nothing. Most assuredly, I say to you, **whatever** you ask the Father in My name He will give you. Until now you have asked nothing in My name. Ask, and you will receive, that your joy may be full."* Hallelujah! When you pray in the name of Jesus, you can have an expectation that God will give you your request and your joy will be full. You don't have to wonder with God; His promises are true. Second Corinthians 1:20 reads, *"For no matter how many promises God has made, they are 'Yes' in Christ. And so through Him the 'Amen' is spoken by us to the glory of God"* (NIV).

When we pray the Word, we're praying His will, and His will is His promise; thus, we can say, "Amen!" *Amen* means, "so be it."[2] It is our agreement that what we've read is what we expect to come to pass in our lives.

The Rewards of Prayer

One of the wonderful attributes of God is He always folds in benefits to our obedience. For instance, "Give and [then] it shall be given" (Luke 6:38 KJV). Keep your mind on Him and (then you will have) peace (see Isa. 26:3). Abide in Me and [then] your joy will be full (see John 15:9-11). Well, prayer is no different. When we pray, there are benefits: Psalm 34:10 says, *"...But those who seek the Lord shall not lack any good thing."* Most of us are familiar with the Matthew 6:33 promise which reads, *"But seek first the kingdom of God and His righteousness, and all these things shall be added to you."* Those things include food, drink, and clothing, and they trail behind a search for God and His ways. With a promise like that, why do we consistently try to acquire those things without God? We attribute higher education, networking with the right people, and success to our own ability, effort, and hard work, but rarely do we consider our obedience to God's promise as the means to obtain things. It's terrible to see Christians espouse the world's outlook on success and lessen or disregard the power of God and His Word. God clearly tells us that the things desired are a byproduct of our prayer life. Matthew 6:26 says, *"Look at the birds of the air; they do not sow or reap or store away in barns, and yet your heavenly Father feeds them. Are you not much more valuable than they?"* (NIV). Those who belong to the Lord seek Him, and in return, He provides for them.

God is all-powerful and all-knowing, and because of that, we can appreciate the other promises too. Matthew 6:6 reads, *"But you, when you pray, go into your room, and when you have shut your door, pray to your Father who is in the secret place; and your Father who sees in secret will reward you openly."* No matter who you are, when God becomes your first, second, and last resort, He will ensure that you rise to the top every time. I'm reminded of King Jehoshaphat's response to the merging enemies. He cried out, (1) We have no power against this great multitude, (2) We don't know what to do, and (3), our eyes are on you (see 2 Chron. 20:12). Not only did King Jehoshaphat look to God, but in reading the Old Testament you'll find king after king consult God regarding His will for Israel when going to war. They never just went to war; they always inquired of the Lord through the prophet of their era. And whenever they listened to the voice of the prophet, they found victory. Likewise, when you look to God as your plan A, plan B, and plan C, He'll navigate you through life with victory. Promises abound in God's Word, but like Israel who was promised the land of milk and honey, we can only receive those promises when we completely trust the One who promised. I mean look at Israel. God promised a land that flowed with milk and honey while other people occupied that land! Yet God removed the unrighteous for His own people, the righteous: *"For exaltation* [promotion] *comes neither from the east nor from the west nor from the south. But God is the Judge: He puts down one, and exalts another"* (Ps. 75:6). Seek God and see impossible doors of opportunity open before you. For those that seek the Lord shall lack for no good thing (see Ps. 34:10).

Benefits of Being With God

In Psalm 37:4, David writes, *"Delight yourself also in the Lord, and He shall give you the desires of your heart."* What an awesome promise God makes us! He's telling us that He cares enough about us to give not just needs but our desires too. The condition is only that we delight in Him. It's an incentive that should prompt us to ask how to delight in the Lord.

As a parent with children getting older, it is a joy to hear stories from their day or hear laughter from their experience. From my interaction with them at those times, I understand a little more what God means by delight in Him. For instance, when my daughter tells me how horrible the lunch in school was and she shares everyone's comments, she laughs and shares her story with so much life. From her story, I not only join in the laughter but I'm ready to make her favorite meal for dinner to compensate for the awful lunch. As it relates to God then, we delight in God when we talk and listen, praise and worship, give and receive. It's the time we use to give attention to the Lord amidst every care and distraction of life that's defined as delight. Those lighthearted, sincere conversations with my children move me to consider ways to bless them. Matthew 7:11 says, *"If you, then, though you are evil, know how to give good gifts to your children, how much more will your Father in heaven give good gifts to those who ask him!"* (NIV).

Delight in Him! Prayer is the interaction with God that shows our delight.

God doesn't mind blessing His people. Just as much as we desire, He desires for us to have. He just doesn't want us to replace our delight in Him with the cares of life. Too often, we go after things first and God says, delight in Me first and then the things will come. *"Seek first His kingdom and His righteousness, and all these things will be given to you as well"* (Matt. 6:33 NIV). When our priorities are skewed, Proverbs 23:5 reads, *"Cast but a glance at riches, and they are gone, for they will surely sprout wings and fly off to the sky like an eagle"* (NIV), but *"He is a rewarder of those who diligently seek Him"* (Heb. 11:6). The diligence mentioned here is our daily and unending attention to God. In fact, this *diligently* in the Greek means "to investigate, search out, crave, demand, and seek after" (Strong's Concordance). That's surely delighting in God when we run after Him with tenacity.

This should be encouraging to us all because there are times when we don't feel like praying, times when we don't feel like our prayers are making a difference or being heard, but it's through these promises that God assures us that our time with Him and our delight in Him is not in vain. And from our time with Him, our relationship with Him is developed and honored.

TEACH ME TO PRAY

"Blessed be the Lord, who daily loads us with benefits, the God of our salvation!" (Ps. 68:19). We shouldn't overlook the benefits of being with our God. We should celebrate them. Many times people talk about how the benefits on their job are so great they would never leave. Even more to the point, I've heard some of these same people talk about the pay not being great, but the benefits are. We should be a people who speak and live the benefits of a life consecrated to God, a life that is committed to the plans of God and a people who delight in the Lord our God.

Another benefit to prayer is found in Psalm 34:5, which reads, *"Those who look to him are radiant; their faces are never covered with shame"* (NIV). Moses is our example of this radiance: *"When Moses came down from Mount Sinai with the two tablets of the Testimony of His hands, he was not aware that his face was radiant because he had spoken with the Lord"* (Exod. 34:29 NIV). Then, *"When Aaron and all the Israelites saw Moses, his face was radiant, and they were afraid to come near him"* (Exod. 34:30 NIV). You see, this radiance was so bright, Exodus 34:35 says, *"they saw his face was radiant. Then Moses would put the veil back over his face until he went in to speak with the Lord"* (NIV). Something happens when you're in the presence of the Lord. His glory comes upon you!

"Arise, shine, for your light has come, and the glory of the Lord rises upon you. See, darkness covers the earth and thick darkness is over the peoples, but the Lord rises upon you and His glory appears over you. Nations will come to your light, and kings to the brightness of your dawn" (Isa. 60:1-3 NIV). If you're a God-seeker, people will look at you strangely sometimes! They will either gravitate toward you or run away from you. They see the light, and while they may not be able to comprehend it, they recognize that you are different: *"For we are to God the aroma of Christ among those who are being saved and those who are perishing. To the one we are the smell of death; to the other, the fragrance of life"* (2 Cor. 2:15-16 NIV). Isn't it wonderful to emit the

fragrance of God? We smell different from the world, and rightly so: *"you are a chosen people, a royal priesthood, a holy nation, a people belonging to God, that you may declare the praises of Him who called you out of darkness into His wonderful light"* (1 Pet. 2:9 NIV).

Delight in His presence and shine—just shine!

Endnotes

1. See http://www.thefreedictionary.com/lifeline.

2. See http://www.studylight.org/lex/heb/view.cgi ?number=0543; "amen."

CHAPTER 5

MY GOD DOES SPEAK

To be in the presence of the Lord offers another great advantage: You have the opportunity to hear from God yourself. It's nice when you go to church and hear a word from the Lord as the pastor or speaker ministers to the congregation—especially when you bear witness that the message was designed just for you. It's encouraging when someone comes with a word from the Lord for you specifically—especially when they pinpoint the exact situation that you're in. To hear from God directly, however, is one of the greatest joys a person can have.

It's a joy many of us forfeit. Innocently, many of us don't often wait to hear from God. We talk but we don't listen. We have a regimented prayer time, but we use the time without giving God a chance to respond. Somehow we've deduced that prayer is one-sided. That's because God is invisible; He is incapable of speaking so that we can hear. This could not be further from the truth. As children of God, we have an ear to hear from Him if we'll take time to listen. John 10:27 says, *"My sheep listen to my voice; I know them and they follow Me"* (NIV). Thus prayer should not be a discourse of life, problems, and cares that is closed with a quick, "Amen." Rather, it should be a dialogue that invites and waits on our God to guide, direct, lead, and answer. In the natural, a conversation with another person that is one-sided would be a conversation most of us would avoid. I remember meeting friends in the cafeteria during college, and every time we gathered there was one person who monopolized the conversation. It wasn't long before we let him know he was a motor-mouth. He never let us get a word in edgewise; it was always an oration. If our time with God is always a monologue rather than a dialogue we'll never get the full benefit of the relationship we can have with Him.

In another scenario, I know someone who did give God a chance to speak, but as soon as she heard God say something she wasn't ready for—good news or otherwise—she simply checked out of the conversation. Incredulously, I asked her why she didn't get everything God said. Her response was simply, "I couldn't handle it." Can you imagine talking to someone who gets up and walks away because he or she doesn't like what you're saying? I wonder what would have happened if Mary had interrupted the Angel Gabriel by getting up, saying, "Thank you, but I don't understand," or "Hey, too heavy," and walking off!

When we dismiss the voice of God, we delay His promises or even jeopardize God's ultimate plan for our lives. If we won't go, we can be replaced. Hearing from God is essential to being in the right place at the right time with the right message. No courier takes wrong messages to wrong businesses and expects a bonus at the end of the year. An efficient courier has clear directions for clear assignments. In turn, he is rewarded for consistency and reliability.

What a fallacy it is to believe that because God is invisible He is unable to speak! What a mistake we can make if we talk to God without taking time to listen! That is not true prayer. To wait on the Lord is a necessary part of our interaction with God. God does have answers. He does give direction, and He knows how to encourage us if we'll let Him speak. We have to determine if our prayers are just therapeutic, or if they are what they're supposed to be: a means of building relationship and obtaining a roadmap for life. God is a living being who cares for and speaks to His children. Moreover, it's in this dialogue called prayer that *"the Lord gives wisdom, and from His mouth come knowledge and understanding"* (Prov. 2:6 NIV).

As young people we were taught to pray saying, "Now I lay me down to sleep, I pray the Lord my soul should keep, and if I should die before I awake, I pray the Lord my soul should take." And, "Thank you for this food that we are about to receive. May it be nourishing to our bodies, in Jesus' name." Many of us were trained to pray using mantras. Trouble is, cute, poetic prayers don't always tell the real and whole story, and we're left at a disadvantage because we're unsure how prayer really works in life.

As a result, our prayer lives can be very limited and artificial. The limitations come from not being able to express from the heart the true issues within, or not making ourselves vulnerable enough to God to receive from Him. The walls we hide behind with people are walls that we can pull down with God. We can rest in the surety of God and His compassion if we'll communicate from the heart. The woman with the issue of blood could have stayed in her home knowing the healer was near, but she chose to break the law (she was technically unclean), press through a throng of people around Jesus, and get her healing. As soon as she touched His clothes, she knew she was healed. Humbling herself even more, as Mark 5:33 records, she *"told him the whole truth"* (NIV). Her decision to lay everything on the line was her decision to know the Christ and receive her healing (see Mark 5:25-34).

Don't let traditions, rules, mistakes, fear, or your shortcomings hinder you from an encounter with God: *"For we do not have a high priest who is unable to sympathize with our weaknesses, but we have one who has been tempted in every way, just as we are—yet was without sin. Let us then approach the throne of grace with confidence, so that we may receive mercy and find grace to help us in our time of need"* (Heb. 4:15-16). When we're stuck in a rut, we cannot see clearly the treasure of our faith. To pray is to comprehend the meaning of Christ's sacrifice and accept the love of the Lord. I recall a time in my life when I made a decision that I knew didn't please God, but rather than run away from Him, I ran to Him. In going to Him, His response was specifically Colossians 1:21-23 which reads,

> *And you, who once were alienated and enemies in your mind by wicked works, yet now He has reconciled in the body of His flesh through death, to present you holy, and blameless, and above reproach in His sight—if indeed you continue in the faith, grounded and steadfast, and are not moved away from the hope of the gospel which you heard, which was preached to every creature under heaven, of which I, Paul, became a minister.*

It was in this response I had a new resolve to not just continue in Christ but to pursue God with greater determination simply because He is God and His kindness to me as seen in that Scripture could not be overlooked. He said, "If I continue," so I made a decision to continue in Him rather than let my mistake take me away from Him.

His love is so utterly amazing.

The Pebble of Sin

Song of Solomon 2:15 tells us to catch the little foxes that spoil the vine. The vine is the relationship we're to have with our Father. John 15:4-5 says, *"Abide in Me, and I in you. As the branch cannot bear fruit of itself, unless it abides in the vine, neither can you, unless you abide in Me. I am the vine, you are the branches. He who abides in Me, and I in him, bears much fruit; for without Me you can do nothing."* Small infractions (foxes) can blight a budding relationship, just as it can destroy a long-lasting one.

A relationship with God enables all of the benefits written in God's Word, but if we don't abide in the vine—if we don't remain in Christ—no matter how small the sin, the relationship can spoil. Thankfully God made provision for the weakness of our flesh. He says, *"if we confess our sins, He is faithful and just and will forgive us our sins and purify us from all unrighteousness"* (1 John 1:9 NIV). This is the ultimate remedy for the mistakes we make in life: repentance.

I live in a commuter's town and quite often there are traffic slowdowns and hour delays. It can be very frustrating when you think you're heading somewhere in a hurry only to get on the turnpike and find standstill traffic. If you're anything like me, it's during those times that you are very thankful for a GPS and you immediately start looking for another way to your destination. There are times, however, when there is no other way. Without repentance, there is no other way to God. Life is like being in a traffic jam; you want to go, but you cannot understand what the hindrance is. With a repentant heart, a standstill life becomes a blessed life.

Prayer is hindered when we justify sin and ignore or postpone repentance. Achan belonged to the Israelites, but when he sinned and took the "accursed things" after God told them to leave the spoil and kill everything, the blessing of victory over their enemies ceased until Joshua dealt with the issue. In fact, God told Joshua that if he didn't deal with the sin, He would no longer be with them to lead them into victory (see Josh. 7:12). When Joshua identified Achan's disobedience, correction was made, and the people of Israel were back on track to fight the enemy and win. When sin is in our lives and there is no repentance, we will never see victories, only defeat. Achan sinned, which caused thirty-six soldiers of Israel to be killed and his whole family stoned. That may be the Old Testament, but there is still a penalty for unrepentant sin today. Romans 6:23 tells us, *"the wages of sin is death, but the gift of God is eternal life in Christ Jesus our Lord"* (NIV).

We have this promise in Second Corinthians 5:19, *"God was in Christ reconciling the world to Himself, not imputing their trespasses to them, and has committed to us the word of reconciliation."* So we can have a relationship with God based on Christ's sacrifice, but we must be very clear that because of His sacrifice, a sinful life comes with consequences. I'm reminded of the sin and rebellion in the life of King David. He prayed Psalm 51 after his fall with Bathsheba. The prophet Nathan came to tell him God was taking away blessings because of his decision to sin. With a repentant heart, David was back on track; he experienced loss, and promises were altered, but he remained king (see 2 Sam. 11-12).

Like a traffic jam can show up around a bend, sin can sneak up on you or emulate a pebble lodged in your shoe which can no longer be ignored. No one else may know a pebble is in your shoe, but eventually like a limp becomes obvious over time, sin increases until it is exposed. God always gives us a chance to judge the sin and correct it before exposure, but if sin is willful and continuous, prayer will be dry and empty because God's waiting for a heart that acknowledges the problem and turns to Him for the answer, for deliverance, for help, and with penance. See, we belong to Him, so He knows us completely: *"O Lord, You have searched me and You know me. You know when I sit and when I rise; You perceive my thoughts from afar. You discern my going out and my lying down; You are familiar with all my ways. Before a word is on my tongue You know it completely, O Lord"* (Ps. 139:1-4 NIV). The knowledge that God has of us is complete; He knows our strengths, and He knows our weaknesses: *"There is no creature hidden from His sight, but all things are naked and open to the eyes of Him to whom we must give account"* (Heb. 4:13). We cannot hide from Him. Our heart is always before Him and while He wants to do good toward us, sin hampers the good He would do.

Jeremiah 5:25 says, *"Your iniquities have turned these things away, and your sins have withheld good from you."* Isaiah prophesies the same message in Isaiah 59:1-2, which reads, *"Behold, the Lord's hand is not shortened, that it cannot save; nor His ear heavy, that it cannot hear. But your iniquities have separated you from your God; and your sins have hidden His face from you, so that He will not hear."* God will always honor His Word, so it's important for those of us who want to be heard to have a heart that is surrendered and submitted to God. This surrender is repentance and it's in repentance that we recognize our need of Him and how much our good works pale in comparison to the shed blood of Jesus Christ.

Therefore, we cry out as David did in Psalm 51:

> *Have mercy upon me, O God, according to your lovingkindness; according to the multitude of your tender mercies, blot out my transgressions. Wash me thoroughly from my iniquity, and cleanse me from my sin.... Purge me with hyssop, and I shall be clean; wash me, and I shall be whiter than snow. Make me hear joy and gladness, that the bones You have broken may rejoice. Hide Your face from my sins, and blot out all my*

iniquities. Create in me a clean heart, O God, and renew a steadfast spirit within me. Do not cast me away from Your presence, and do not take Your Holy Spirit from me. Restore to me the joy of Your salvation, and uphold me by Your generous Spirit. Then I will teach transgressors Your ways, and sinners shall be converted to You (Psalm 51:1-3;7-13).

A repentant heart can make all the difference in how we receive from God. When sin is in our lives, we cannot buy God's favor. We cannot manipulate God; He isn't interested in our sacrifices and our offerings. At the point of sin God is only interested in you: *"The Lord is not slack concerning His promise, as some count slackness, but is longsuffering toward us, not willing that any should perish but that all should come to repentance"* (2 Pet. 3:9). You may not see blessings or answers to prayer come as you wanted, but one thing you can be assured of, God is available to you if you will humble yourself, renounce your sin, and turn to Him. Psalm 51:16-17 says, *"For You delight not in sacrifice, or else would I give it; You find no pleasure in burnt offering. My sacrifice [the sacrifice acceptable] to God is a broken spirit; a broken and a contrite heart [broken down with sorrow for sin and humbly and thoroughly penitent], such, O God, You will not despise"* (AMP). I think the The Message translation of this passage helps us even more: *"Going through the motions doesn't please You, a flawless performance is nothing to You. I learned God-worship when my pride was shattered. Heart-shattered lives ready for love don't for a moment escape God's notice."*

His awesome display of love is the safety net we all need to come back into the fold. There is penalty for sin, but a changed heart can salvage God's purpose, plans, and promises in your life. More than anything, it can open His ear to your cry once again.

CHAPTER 6

THE CHANGED HEART

Before I gave my life to Christ I found a way to be stoic about many things that moved other people emotionally. After Christ, I permitted my heart to feel and express outwardly what was changed inwardly. It was very liberating, though I didn't consciously make that decision. Looking back, I recall a gentleman who knew me before Christ commenting how much I changed outwardly after Christ. He spoke freely and looked quite surprised with my overall appearance. At the time I thought he was weird, but at this point I understand better what the work of Christ can do in the heart of any person yielded to Him. Moreover, I believe that work can transform us outwardly. (See Mark 5:15 as an example.)

The change after repentance is within the heart. People usually make adjustments in behavior and habits after coming to Christ, but without that changed heart those adjustments are short-lived and based on sheer willpower. With the changed heart, however, the will of humanity is turned from selfish desires and false motives to a desire based on sincerely pleasing God.

I remember a clown who had his face painted, just like you would expect. He wore the brightly colored wig and the colorful clown suite. He even acted like you would have expected. He danced around smiling with the painted smile and interacted with the children like only a clown would. He was quite animated and comical. Afterward, when the excitement around the clown ended, I saw a plain-clothed person heading to his car; he was the clown. The difference was remarkable. Not only did he look hard and disinterested, but his conversation was now flat and dry. And while he wasn't completely cold, he definitely was not inviting. I give this example to bring to our attention how easy it is to be someone or something outwardly when in fact inwardly we are completely different. This clown did his job for which he got paid and he left. As Christians however, we don't get paid to act. We are Christians because of our acceptance of Christ and from that acknowledgment we're growing more and more like Him. This inward growth is what breaks the façade we've built over the years. If we choose to act like the clown, however, we may fool people but we'll never fool God. He knows the heart of everyone.

Jeremiah 17:9-10 reads, *"The heart is deceitful above all things, and desperately wicked; who can know it? I, the Lord, search the heart, I test the mind, even to give every man according to his ways, according to the fruit of his doings."* Notice the connection between our heart and our receiving of blessings or answers to prayers. When our heart is right, God doesn't withhold from us. In fact Psalm 84:11 reads, *"For the Lord God is a sun and shield; the Lord bestows favor and honor; no good thing does He withhold from those whose walk is blameless"* (NIV).

The key then to answered prayer is found within my heart. The New Living Translation says it like this, *"But I the Lord, search all hearts and examine secret motives. I give all people their due rewards, according to what their actions deserve"* (Jer. 17:10 NLT). With this in mind, we must be prepared to really examine our own hearts. First Corinthians 11:31-32 says, *"But if we judged ourselves, we would not come under judgment. When we are judged by the Lord, we are being disciplined so that we will not be condemned with the world"* (NIV). Isn't it always better to self-critique than listen to someone else critique you? I encourage all of us to judge our sin, repent, and cry out to God for a clean heart.

Prayer is not the time to excuse bad behavior and ignore real shortcomings. It's not the time to say, "I know this is a problem, but...." With God, remove the "but," and allow His hand to provide deliverance. It is during your time with God that what's on the inside—good, bad, and ugly— should be exposed. He is an All-consuming fire, and He will burn up the chaff in our lives (see Luke 3:16-18).

Once we've judged our sins and surrendered to the Lord our God, Second Timothy 2:22 says, *"Flee the evil desires of youth, and pursue righteousness, faith, love and peace, along with those who call on the Lord out of a pure heart"* (NIV). Our call to God should be out of a pure heart, untainted by the world and its ways, uncontaminated with doubt and unbelief. No corrosion. God doesn't take away all bad behavior miraculously; He expects us to fear Him and shun evil (see Prov. 3:7). He tells us to wash our hands and purify our hearts (see James 4:8 NIV). We're purifying ourselves from the double-minded ways with which we approach God.

The double-mindedness is seen when we say we believe, but we don't act like we believe (see Matt. 23:15). We say we love God, but we're not obedient to God (see John 14:23). We go to church, but we don't do what we're taught when we leave (see James 1:22-25). This double nature is not God's way. He wants us to be single minded and unpolluted so we may be His children in singleness of heart.

This is what God told the prophet Jeremiah regarding the people: *"They will be My people, and I will be their God. I will give them singleness of heart and action, so that they will always fear Me for their own good and the good of their children after them...I will never stop doing good to them, and I will inspire them to fear Me, so that they will never turn away from Me"* (Jer. 32:38-40 NIV). That's His promise. Will you cooperate with His plan? To cooperate is to surrender— no longer resisting God's ways, plans, and purposes, but committing to live life His way.

Run to God!

While we strive for perfection, God's grace upholds us (see Matt. 5:48). Never think you cannot go to God because of sin or because of challenges in life. When we sin, the enemy condemns us into thinking we should stay away from God, His people, church, etc. Never run away from God; run to Him! He's not waiting for us to live life perfectly and precisely before He welcomes us and aids or rescues us. He aids and rescues people who recognize they cannot make it without Him. He responds to people who turn to Him without any more options; God wants to be our source for everything, not just a resource when needed. He wants to be the rock that we turn to. Jeremiah was told to tell the people, *"Call to Me, and I will answer you, and show you great and mighty things, which you do not know"* (Jer. 33:3).

Don't dismiss the power of prayer. Don't discount the hand of God in your situation. Don't assume the invisible is the non-existent and you can do whatever you want and still be heard by God. Prayer does work if we trust Him completely. Trusting means relying, and relying means being dependent enough to live life as required by His Word. There, in that place of obedience, God answers prayer.

To give you a simple example, I teach a Seniors Bible Study and each time I teach I ask God to help me. Simple right? Well, there are times when God tells me to read certain Scriptures during my time with Him, and I have a choice to follow His leading or reject it. I could reject because I'm tired, late, or any other excuse, or I can listen by being obedient. On more than one occasion, I have listened and found our study so much more complete because the very Scriptures God was leading me to read were the Scriptures my Seniors needed for those impromptu discussions or unplanned questions. I tell you it's wonderful to obey God, because when He tells us to do something it means we can do it and it means our obedience will bless us or another.

CHAPTER 7

I PLEDGE ALLEGIANCE

Second Timothy 2:13 tells us, *"…if we are faithless, He will re-main faithful"* (NIV). Faithfulness means to be unwavering and consistent. Too often we allow things around us to sway and/or distract our resolve to continue in Him and His Word. We start well, but our endurance can be challenging. The promise we have in Second Timothy is that regardless of how much we fluctuate, God remains faithful to His own.

While there are many Scriptures that speak to the faithfulness of God, we also can find Scripture that encourages us to be just as faithful to God as He is to us. Proverbs 28:20 offers an incentive that I particularly appreciate. It reads, *"A faithful man will abound with blessings."* Along with incentives to remain faithful to God, we see scriptural examples of those who were not faithful to God and their end result.

The Israelites are an excellent example because, while they experienced the faithfulness of God, we see their waywardness and the results therein. In fact, it was because of their faithlessness that Israel found themselves oppressed by other nations on more than one occasion. In fact, as much as the children of Israel were delivered because of the faithfulness of God, they found themselves dominated by other nations because their response to God was fickle. In Judges 3:12-15 we're given the historic account that helps us to see how disloyal Israel was.

> *And the children of Israel again did evil in the sight of the Lord. So the Lord strengthened Eglon king of Moab against Israel, because they had done evil in the sight of the Lord. Then he gathered to himself the people of Ammon and Amalek, went and defeated Israel, and took possession of the City of Palms. So the children of Israel served Eglon king of Moab eighteen years. But when the children of Israel cried out to the Lord, the Lord raised up a deliverer for them...* (Judges 3:12-15).

Now with this and several other accounts where Israel is subject to another nation, you would say that God didn't prove Himself faithful, but He actually did. For one, His main reasons for allowing other nations to take Israel captive was *"because this nation has transgressed My covenant which I commanded their fathers, and has not heeded My voice, I also will no longer drive out before them any of the nations which Joshua left when he died, so that through them I may test Israel, whether they will keep the ways of the Lord to walk in them as their fathers kept them, or not. Therefore the Lord left those nations without driving them out immediately; nor did He deliver them into the hand of Joshua"* (Judges 2:20-23). So, we see God is so committed to us that He's willing to let us make a decision that could hinder or jeopardize various blessings until we're clear and sure that He is God and our loyalty is toward Him. In His faithfulness, He has an expectation that His children will also be faithful to Him. And while consequences abound toward us just as it did for Israel, it's in the faithfulness of God that He came to their rescues each time Israel called upon Him with a repentant heart. They cried out and God came to their rescue.

In fact, no matter how badly they sinned against God, they always ran to Him, and God was always there for them. Regardless of what they did, God always answered them. In Judges chapter 6, we're told the Israelites are greatly impoverished because of their bondage to Midian for seven years. They cry out to God and He chastises them (see Judg. 6:7-10), but He also begins to put their deliverance plan in place by calling Gideon. They were the product of God's favor, and once again they saw their Deliverer come through for them. God is faithful, so Israel experienced His hand of mercy and favor continuously. God's promise to Abraham was fulfilled as He multiplied them, led them out of Egyptian bondage, parted seas, and gave them sustenance at request. From their water, the manna, and the meat, God took care of them.

And God has taken care of you too. While it is easy to rehash hurts and disappointments, we must also recognize the many instances when God intervened in our lives. Circumstances may not have been perfect, but if we take time to track our lives, we can identify the grace and favor of God that has kept us to this very moment. We're here because the hand of God upheld us, not because of personal effort or savvy.

In all situations, then, it's important to recognize that He is our Keeper (see Ps. 121:5) and His presence is what makes the difference in life. Before going to college, I remember reading a Scripture that spoke about God keeping me away from evil people. I didn't know Him very well, and how I found that Scripture was quite the miracle. I never read my Bible, and on that day I just thumbed there and it caught my attention. My prayer was simple, and I underlined those words in that Bible. From that quick prayer, I can track those dumb days in college when He did indeed keep me away from evil people and protect me from potentially dangerous situations. God was faithful in my life when I didn't know enough to serve Him with my whole heart. I'm sure if you look at your life, you can see the faithfulness of God.

Israel wasn't anymore perfect than we are. From Scripture, we are shown a people who had the same temperamental attitude that many of us have today. Before the Red Sea parted, they were afraid (see Exod. 14:10). When Moses wasn't around, they lost their focus (see Exod. 32:1), when they became thirsty or hungry, they grumbled and complained (Exod. 15:24). When it took too long to get to the promise land, they second-guessed Moses' authority (Numbers 16:3). They expressed their heart on a number of occasions even when their heart was less than pure. Yet God continued to be faithful to the children of Israel. He *"went ahead of them in a pillar of cloud to guide them on their way and by night in a pillar of fire to give them light, so that they could travel day or night. Neither the pillar of cloud by day nor the pillar of fire by night left its place in front of the people"* (Exod. 13:21-22 NIV). We can all be thankful that God's faithfulness abounds toward us as well.

The difference between Israel and the church today—that would be you and me—is we have the opportunity to develop a true relationship with Him, whereas Israel was satisfied with receiving from His hand alone. Psalm 103:7 says, *"He made known His ways to Moses, His deeds to the people of Israel"* (NIV). As a people, Israel only knew God through the representatives who sought Him continually on their behalf, like Moses or Joshua. Consequently, Israel witnessed God's saving power and experienced His provision, but they failed to interact with Him personally.

In fact, the one time God spoke to Israel as a way to endorse Moses (see Exod. 19:9) it was so traumatic they begged Moses to speak to God alone: *"When the people saw the thunder and lightning and heard the trumpet and saw the mountain in smoke, they trembled with fear. They stayed at a distance and said to Moses, 'Speak to us yourself and we will listen. But do not have God speak to us or we will die'"* (Exod. 20:18-20 NIV).

Being afraid of God didn't lend itself to a strong relationship with God. Instead of being obedient, compliant, and reverent after deliverance, they typically went back to their faithless ways.

This doesn't have to be our lot. Other people, situations, and problems should not dominate our lives. We serve a God who is available to us and willing to help no matter who we are and what our past has been. He comes to our rescue just as He came to Israel's rescue when they called upon Him. Our response to the deliverance He provides should, however, be different from Israel. While they defected until they needed help, we should call on God and begin developing a relationship with Him that's beyond our needs but based on our sincere desire to be consistent and unwavering in our allegiance to Him. From Israel's example, we may have a fear of Him that begins with trepidation; but from a developed relationship, this fear is a reverence of and commitment to Him. Hebrews 4:16 says, *"Let us therefore come boldly to the throne of grace, that we may obtain mercy and find grace to help in time of need."* Now we have the opportunity to approach God any time we want without apprehension but with confidence in His faithfulness for an unending relationship.

The relationship I'm speaking of is developed through time with our Father. That time begins in His Word, but from His Word comes our time in His presence. Thus, relationship building is when we set aside time to fellowship with our Father and when we're obedient to what His Word says. I encourage you to remove distractions and, yes, responsibilities to seek God, hear from God, reason with God, understand God, and know God. He doesn't tell us to come to Him as perfect people. His desire is simply that we come. If an hour is too much for you now, start with ten minutes, but just start somewhere. Make a decision to seek God for who He is, not because there is a need in your life or a concern before you, but because your desire is to be sincere and genuine in a relationship that was begun when Jesus Christ was received as a Savior and Lord. *"'Come now, let us reason together,' says the Lord, 'Though your sins are like scarlet, they shall be as white as snow; though they are red as crimson, they shall be like wool. If you are willing and obedient, you will eat the best from the land'"* (Isa. 1:18-19 NIV).

God is interested in a people who serve Him when things are well or call on Him when trouble abounds; He is interested in people who call on Him as the representatives of Israel did: consistently, obediently, and sincerely. When we are faithfully committed to God, we are building a relationship that affords the promise of His hand of grace and favor upon our lives.

CHAPTER 8

OBEDIENCE FOR RESULTS

Obedience is the state in which we, as Christians, should remain if we want our prayers to be effective. Obedience is not subjective. It's not based on convenience, how we feel, what we think, or the way we rationalize our decisions. Obedience is doing exactly what is directed, whether we understand it or not. When we say that we love God but excuse our disobedience to Him, we are duplicitous in heart. That duplicity hinders prayer and gives the oppressions of life a season pass in every area of life.

While I would love to tell everyone reading this book that your prayers can never be hindered, the Bible says they can (see Ps. 66:18;

Luke 18:14; James 1:6; 4:3,6). Disobedience will hinder or even deny the answers to your prayers. I must qualify this statement by sharing an observation. We're all at different levels in our spiritual development, just as we're all at different ages and maturity levels naturally. What I could get away with as a five year old would not necessarily work as a ten year old. Likewise, as a new believer, you will find that God answers prayers immediately. He proves Himself to you as a God you can trust and rely upon. As you mature spiritually, you'll find answers to prayer require a little more from your end, like using the Word (as referenced earlier in "The Template of His Word"), like using your faith, and confessing sin, and even more, like obedience. I've heard of one person getting healed by the promise and power of God following her salvation, and I've seen a seasoned Christian fight to receive his promised healing year after year. There are stages of development, and God has expectations of us in these varying stages (see Heb. 5:12-13; 6:1-2).

This obedience doesn't just involve going to church or reading your Bible; obedience in other areas is necessary too. For example, I love the story of the widow woman in First Kings 17. There is a famine in the land, and Elijah is told to visit a widow woman in Zarephath. When Elijah arrives, he asks her for food. She says she's gathering sticks for her and her child's last meal (see 1 Kings 17:10). Yet, in First Kings 17:9, God tells Elijah, *"Go at once to Zarephath of Sidon and stay there. I have commanded a widow in that place to supply you with food."* Think about that. This woman was commanded to feed the prophet before the prophet's arrival. She was commanded just as the ravens were "ordered to feed" Elijah (see 1 Kings 17:4). Maybe she was told to feed him when things were easy, so she agreed—or maybe she was told to feed him when things started looking bleak. We don't know when God gave her this command, but once the prophet arrived, she had to decide between obedience and disobedience, logic and faith, trust and doubt.

Thankfully, she chose obedience to God: *"She went away and did as Elijah had told her"* (1 Kings 17:15). The result: *"So there was food every day for Elijah and for the woman and her family. For the jar of flour was not used up and the jug of oil did not run dry, in keeping with the word of the Lord spoken by Elijah"* (1 Kings 17:15-16).

Obedience is just as important as having expectation. Obviously this woman had a relationship with God because she heard Him give directions about a soon-coming prophet. In response to her relationship, she obeyed and found out that God was not trying to hurt her by telling her to give up the last of the oil and flour; He was saving her. Trust is another component of relationship. We won't always understand why God directs us to do certain things, but because we're in relationship with Him, we know that He has our best interest in mind.

Honoring Our Relationship

Our decision to obey His voice or scriptural direction is a decision to honor the relationship that we have with Him. His greatest request is that we love Him, and loving God is being obedient to God. Deuteronomy 11:1 says, *"Therefore you shall love the Lord your God, and keep His charge, His statutes, His judgments, and His commandments always."* In this chapter, God positions us to be blessed if we choose to obey Him (see Deut. 11:13-17;22-25) and cursed if we decide *not* to obey (see Deut. 11:28). The choice to obey or disobey is our own. The widow at Zarephath chose to obey, and in so doing, she received the blessing. Had she excused herself from obedience because she resented Elijah's insensitivity to her plight, she would have died accordingly.

Many times we're told to do things that we don't understand. It doesn't make sense, and it's just not convenient; yet, when God speaks to us, it's important for us to honor the relationship, believing the best of Him and believing in His faithfulness toward us. When you ask God for something, don't dismiss His answer. It may very well have everything to do with your request. God is never on a tangent; He's speaking your answer. You'll realize it when you obey.

I recall hearing a teacher of the Gospel tell of his need for a plane. He asked God to replace his plane, and he immediately heard God ask him to give away various suits in his closet. Though he didn't want to give away his suits, he did, and his plane followed soon after. My Bishop, Dr. I.V. Hilliard, testified about the need for a new engine in his plane. He prayed and God's response was for him to give a significant offering in another pastor's church. With his obedience came his new engine.

Obedience doesn't have to make sense; we simply decide to trust that what God asks us to do is for our benefit and the possible benefit of another. I love the fact that though we're limited, God is able to declare the end from the beginning (see Isa. 46:10). The One who knows all things knows what is good for us. He answered the prayer of the Israelites and brought them out of Egyptian bondage by way of the wilderness. They didn't understand what God was doing, but God was completely aware of every circumstance: *"Then it came to pass, when Pharaoh had let the people go, that God did not lead them by way of the land of the Philistines, although that was near; for God said, 'Lest perhaps the people change their minds when they see war, and return to Egypt.' So God led the people around by way of the wilderness of the Red Sea. And the children of Israel went up in orderly ranks out of the land of Egypt"* (Exod. 13:17-18). Though Israel complained throughout most of the journey, we can see that God knew what was best for them. He preferred to separate the Red Sea so the people could cross on dry ground (see Exod. 14:16) rather than have them fearful and running back to familiar oppression.

If we're not careful, we'll miss the blessings of God because we're choosing to lean on our own logic and reason: *"Trust in the Lord with all your heart and lean not on your own understanding; in all your ways acknowledge Him, and He shall direct your paths"* (Prov. 3:5-6).

CHAPTER 9

PRAYER IS
SPIRITUAL LOGIC

Prayer is your spiritual logic. Praying about a situation or an issue may not make sense to anyone but you because you have chosen to place your hope in Him. The God we serve says that when His people seek Him, He'll not only deliver and honor them (see Ps. 91:15), but He'll also give grace and glory (see Ps. 84:11). The ways of God defy our reasoning. It may not make sense to go into your room and shut the door and seek His face when the cabinets are empty, but it sure will make the difference. It may not make sense to excuse yourself from a meeting so you can get the mind of Christ, but it sure will make the difference. It may not make sense to offer undignified praise during sadness, but it sure will make a difference. Prayer is our spiritual logic.

With prayer as a lifestyle, Daniel went into the lion's den and came out saying, *"O King live forever! My God sent His angel, and He shut the mouths of the lions. They have not hurt me, because I was found innocent in His sight"* (Dan. 6:21-22 NIV). With spiritual logic, Hannah sought the Lord and He *"remembered her. So in the course of time Hannah conceived and gave birth to a son. She named him Samuel, saying, 'Because I asked the Lord for him'"* (1 Sam. 1:19-20 NIV). Prayer defies human logic, but when you experience God's answer, you'll find it makes perfect spiritual sense.

I was talking to a lady, and in the conversation she complained of carpel tunnel syndrome. She mentioned it in passing because the pain was worsening and she now believed it may be time to pursue the surgery she had long put off. I heard the Lord say to pray for her. In obedience I did, and God became her physician. She squeezed my hand several times surprised that God had met her need. She felt no pain. Logic of the world would have led me to encourage her to pursue her doctors, to wear a brace, or to consider other options before such invasive surgery, but the God we pray to was prepared to meet her need through my simple act of obedience.

Fleece or Faith

Let's return to the Israelites' story in Judges 6. When Israel cried out to God for deliverance, God heard them, and the Angel of the Lord appeared to a young man named Gideon as he threshed wheat in the winepress *"in order to hide it from the Midianites"* (Judg. 6:11). The Angel of the Lord greeted Gideon with these words: *"The Lord is with you, you mighty man of valor!"* (Judge 6:12). What an odd way to greet Gideon, who certainly did not appear to be a man of war or valor! He boldly asked this guest about the current state of affairs that the God of their history based on their current predicament: *"O my lord, if the Lord is with us, why then has all this happened to us?"* (Judge 6:13). How often have you said this as a Christian? Maybe you didn't articulate it, but you thought about it. If God is with me and I'm so blessed, why is my situation so over-whelming? Gideon was as curious about his situation as you may be about yours. He was unable to reconcile the contradiction of his new title or God's silence concerning his people. So he continues by asking, *"And where are all His miracles which our fathers told us about, saying, 'Did not the Lord bring us up from Egypt?'"* (Judg. 6:13). His question is reasonable since he's heard great stories of deliverance. *"But now the Lord has forsaken us and delivered us into the hands of the Midianites"* (Judg. 6:13).

I put Gideon in the category of those who may be apathetic to God. You don't mind going to church, but life's contradictions hinder complete commitment or zeal for God. Thus going to church is more out of trained respect rather than reverent awe. Gideon knew of God through the stories told by his foremothers and fathers (see Judg. 6:13). He heard about the Red Sea experience; he heard about bread falling from the sky; he heard about God; but He didn't have a personal experience and could only base God's existence, love, and relevance on his current state of bondage, hardship, and grief.

Maybe you heard your grandmother talk about His faithfulness, you saw your relatives serve in church, and you adopted the tradition of church attendance with dedicated involvement, but inwardly you're like Gideon, unsure. You may pray, but you're not always convinced it's God speaking, so it's easy to ignore the directives given. You have a relationship with God, but you're not invested enough to act upon what you know. You're being safe, resting upon the laurels of those before you, rather than living obediently before your God.

Remember, prayer is your spiritual lifeline. And the same God that revealed Himself to Gideon is the God who can reveal Himself to you. Moreover, it's in the revelation of who He is in your life that you can be who God calls you, just as Gideon, and you can do things that supersede humankind's opinion and society's assumption of you while He affirms Himself in your life as the same God yesterday, today, and forever.

If you begin using your faith to pray, God can meet you where you are. Questions are not too hard for God, though they may be His opportunity to show Himself strong in your life. Let your questions be submitted to Him in prayer and your heart surrendered enough to respond when He answers. Gideon heard from God, but his heart wouldn't allow him to submit until a fleece was made to confirm God's will for his life. Thomas also required a sort of fleece when he declared he wouldn't believe until he saw the nail marks and put his finger in Jesus' side, and while his fleece was honored Jesus told him, *"You believe because you see, but blessed are those who have not seen and yet have believed"* (see John 20:29 NIV).

Don't rely on a fleece when you can will yourself to believe what is written and believe in the God who is there for you. When a fleece is made it's based on a heart that must be convinced before a willingness to accept is made. God isn't pleased when we don't believe because, again, He desires a relationship where we can trust Him, and trust His motives toward us are for our benefit and well-being.

Agreeing With God

Zechariah is another person who needed more than the Word of God before he could accept what was being said to him. He was a priest unto God, which should mean he had a relationship with God, but after receiving a divine visit from an angel regarding the birth of his child, John (later to be called John the Baptist), he opened his mouth saying, *"How can I be sure of this? I am an old man and my wife is well along in years"* (Luke 1:18 NIV). He did more than ask for a fleece; he gave place to doubt. His question was insulting and the angel's response seems terse. *"I am Gabriel. I stand in the presence of God, and I have been sent to speak to you and to tell you this good news"* (Luke 1:19 NIV). As a priest, Zechariah should have been more sensitive to spiritual matters, yet he missed the significance of the message and the messenger; as a result, he was sentenced to silence until the words Gabriel spoke came to pass (see Luke 1:20 NIV).

Mary, the mother of Jesus, received a visit with equally puzzling news, yet her response wasn't couched in doubt as Zechariah's was; instead, she asked, *"How will this be…since I am a virgin?"* (Luke 1:34). She didn't second-guess the angel's words; she simply asked how it would happen. Zechariah asked, "How will I know?" Essentially, he's saying that logically, he cannot be sure God is able to override facts that scream, "Impossible!" It's the same as telling your child, "I'm going to take you to school tomorrow," and the child asks, "But how will I know?" Most of us would be disappointed that the child needed another context to accept our words. As a matter of fact, most of us would respond quite quickly with, "You know because I told you!" If the child asked instead, "How will you do that since you normally leave before me?" we would explain our changed plans. The difference is in what you are willing to accept. If you can look at God's Word and accept what He has promised, you may not understand how it can happen, but a willingness to receive is certainly different from another who may read the Word of God and decide not to believe it because it's not logical or doesn't appear to be possible based on factual information. Mary yielded to the angels report, though the fact was she was still a virgin. She accepted the report saying, *"I am the Lord's servant…may it be to me as you have said"* (Luke 1:38 NIV). And because of her acceptance, the supernatural took place.

Zechariah was silenced because of his doubt. Isn't it interesting that the angel chose to close his mouth? This is the case with Zechariah, but it is something that many of us should volunteer to do after we've prayed and received God's promise. If we're not going to speak in agreement with what God has promised, it's better not to say anything at all.

Faith is an action word, and faith is released by the words of our mouth. Therefore, to use my faith, I have to be very careful what comes out of my mouth. If I believe then my words should consistently speak what I believe. If I believe Jesus is Lord on Sunday, I should be able to say He's Lord throughout the week because I believe it. What we say indicates what we truly believe. If I can consistently say Jesus is Lord, whether the sun is shining or the skies are cloudy, whether I'm happy or sad, then I am convinced. In good or troubled times, if Jesus remains Lord, it's safe to say that I believe it. Likewise with His promises, if I believe that *all my needs are met according to His riches in glory by Christ Jesus* (see Phil. 4:19), I must continue saying His truth even when the presented facts contradict my confession. That is faith.

As you pray, use your faith. Make a decision to believe God based on His promise and resolve to continue in His Word regardless of how you feel and what things look like. To do that means you must stay in the presence of God so you will continue to say what He has said concerning your life.

Hebrews 10:19-24 tells us how we should enter the presence of God, or pray: *"So, friends, we can now—without hesitation—walk right up to God, into 'the Holy Place.' Jesus has cleared the way by the blood of His sacrifice, acting as our priest before God. The 'curtain' into God's presence is His body. So let's do it—full of belief, confident that we're presentable inside and out. Let's keep a firm grip on the promises that keep us going. He always keeps His word"* (TM). The last line is my greatest admonishment: *"keep a firm grip on the promises"* (Heb. 10:23 TM). Don't weaken your resolve; stand strong.

"Now may the God of hope fill you with all joy and peace in believing, that you may abound in hope by the power of the Holy Spirit" (Rom. 15:13). May you be *"strengthened with all might, according to His glorious power for all patience and longsuffering with joy"* (Col. 1:11). And may you stand strong in the faith knowing He who promised is faithful (see Heb. 10:23).

As much as you want to know God, He wants you to know Him more. He is always available to you, and if you will present yourself before Him, He'll not only make known Himself to you, but you'll see the correlation between His confirmation and your decision to pray. Your faith may not be strong, but God is strong.

Matthew 5:6 says, *"Blessed are those who hunger and thirst for righteousness, for they will be filled"* (NIV).

CHAPTER 10

A RIGHT-NOW GOD

When we call on God, we can have an expectation that He is always available to us regardless of the hour, the occasion, or our state of being.

For instance, if a child scraped his knee, we wouldn't wait to deal with the tears, the broken heart, or the actual bruise; our love would compel an immediate response. There is no delay with God either. We have what we ask when we pray: *"Therefore I tell you, whatever you ask for in prayer, believe that you have received it, and it will be yours"* (Mark 11:24 NIV). This verse doesn't say, "Believe that you have received it when you see it materialize." The Scripture says that you should believe you have what you ask when you pray, the *moment* you pray. If you can believe that you have it when you pray, then it will be yours. James 5:16 reads, *"The effective, fervent prayer of the righteous man avails much."* Pray with purpose, intention, and expectation.

Jesus taught this principle, and we would do well to accept it. If after you've prayed, you "doubt that you'll get the answer," you've missed it. Our unwillingness to believe that we have what we've prayed for when we prayed means we'll never receive it—then or later.

In the various stories of people who needed Jesus' help for themselves or their children in Matthew's Gospel, the people came to Jesus and worshiped Him saying what they knew Jesus was capable of doing, not what they doubted He could do. Too often we go to God defeated. We don't suppose God can heal, so we pray a quick end. We're not sure He can provide, so we just want God to make a relative lend us the money upon request. Yet, when these people came to Jesus, they came with an expectation that they would receive what they asked and that He was the only one who could answer their care or concern. They used the faith that saw the end of the matter in their favor rather than doubt that saw the matter as it was.

My goal is to help you pray effectively. So when you pray, believing God's promise is imperative to answers. Believing doesn't mean to keep asking for the same thing each night. If I keep asking for it night after night, it means I never received it the first time, or the second time, or each night I repeat the prayer. If my child asked me for a pencil and I gave her one, she wouldn't continue to stand there asking me for a pencil. She would thank me and depart. If she doesn't believe it's a pencil in her hand after asking the first time, however, she would ask again. If she receives the pencil, though, I would expect her to say "thank you." Likewise, if you receive your answer when you prayed, then your only response should be, "Thank you." Not because you see it in the natural, but because you believe His Word of promise. Therefore, when we receive by faith, we should begin to give thanks for the answer to the request made. It matters not how long you've said *thank you* for the answer, keep on thanking Him. Healing? Keep thanking Him. Restoration? Keep thanking Him. Deliverance? Keep thanking Him. If the problem keeps announcing itself, you keep thanking God for the change. Thank Him—not that it's *going* to change—but that it *has* changed.

Faith is now: *"Now faith is the substance of things hoped for, the evidence of things not seen"* (Heb. 11:1). Faith isn't tomorrow; faith is now. The faith that I use when I pray is the faith that enables me to receive my request. My resolve to hold onto God's Word as my promise determines how long I'll have to stand. Bishop I.V. Hilliard says if you're willing to wait a lifetime for what you believe, you won't have to believe a lifetime to receive. This is faith at work. As an encouragement, Hebrews 10:35 says, *"Therefore do not cast away your confidence, which has great reward. For you have need of endurance, so that after you have done the will of God, you may receive the promise."*

Our God is a right-now God. And while you may want to give up, while you're tempted to toss in the towel and declare God didn't come through for you, I encourage you to *"Hold fast* [to your] *confession. For we do not have a High Priest who cannot sympathize with our weaknesses, but was in all points tempted as we are, yet without sin. Let us therefore come boldly to the throne of grace, that we may obtain mercy and find grace to help in time of need"* (Heb. 4:14b-16).

When you feel weak in your resolve to believe, pray! You're experiencing the temptation that God has already given you the victory over. Temptation is anything that would take you away from truth (God's Word). Go to God and get His wisdom, that being, how to fear God in the situation before you. When you ask Him for wisdom, He'll give it to you without finding fault. More than that, He'll extend His mercy (compassion) and grace (unmerited favor) to help you for that time of need.

CHAPTER 11

POSITION YOURSELF

When you tug on the spiritual lifeline and you're being pulled to safety, it's not time to wiggle or resist the moving cord. You must position yourself. Jehoshaphat positioned himself by worshiping God. You worship when you know God has come through for you. You worship with thanksgiving because you are relieved. You worship God when you know the situation is in His control.

For Jehoshaphat, the positioning took place before the actual victory materialized. Jehoshaphat and the people began to praise *before* they saw a vanquished enemy. They worshiped and praised God before they went out on the field at God's directive, and that's what we must do if we're going to be in position to see the victory materialize. When we get in position, we celebrate and worship. We announce the answer and praise God for the victory. When the storms of life seem to rage stronger, we praise louder; when the problem seems to get bigger, we remain in a posture of thanksgiving. Giving thanks for what we've already asked for is worship. During worship and praise, we can stand still and see the salvation of the Lord in our lives just as Jehoshaphat did. When you're in position, you don't waver; you don't change your opinion; you don't withdraw your trust; you simply believe.

In the natural, it didn't make sense for Jehoshaphat to lead the people in adoration of God; he should have been counting his men and sharpening his swords. Instead, he worshiped God by walking according to spiritual logic—obedience. He had a word, and from it he was able to encourage those around him: *"Hear me, O Judah and you inhabitants of Jerusalem: Believe in the Lord your God, and you shall be established; believe His prophets, and you shall prosper"* (2 Chron. 20:20).

Jehoshaphat saw his enemies rallying against him, and he turned to the Lord praying and praising God. Jehoshaphat didn't stop there. He petitioned God's help and then humbled himself declaring his state: *"We have no power against this great multitude that is coming against us;" "nor do we know what to do,"* and finally, *"but our eyes are upon you"* (2 Chron. 20:12). Then God spoke through His servant Jahaziel, *"in the midst of the assembly: ... 'Do not be afraid nor dismayed because of this great multitude, for the battle is not yours, but God's.... You will not need to fight in this battle. Position yourselves, stand still and see the salvation of the Lord, who is with you, O Judah and Jerusalem! Do not fear or be dismayed; tomorrow go out against them, for the Lord is with you'"* (2 Chron. 20:14-17).

I tell you, Jehoshaphat received good news. He turned to the Lord, and the Lord heard the cry of the people and came to their defense.

My sister and brother, you have good news too. Seek the face of God. It matters not who you are. When you call on Him, He will answer you and show you great and mighty things which you do not know (see Jer. 33:3 NIV). So position yourself. Have faith in God expecting results.

CHAPTER 12

HOLY SPIRIT AND YOU

Until this point, you have prayed from your heart and with the Word of God. These two ways yield return from God, but they can be limiting to what we know and what we are learning. Yet, there is a way to pray beyond our understanding that affords great value, and that is praying in the Holy Spirit.

As Christians, we embrace the Trinity: God the Father, God the Son, and God the Holy Spirit. And while we accept the Scripture references for Holy Spirit, far too many of us have not appreciated His personal role in our lives. For some, we simply don't know who He is, so He's of no consequence. For others, we've heard so many different reports that we make no mention of Him lest we error in judgment. And then there are others who reject Holy Spirit because of their experience and/or assumptions.

As Christians, however, it's important for us to understand who the third person of the Trinity is and accept what the Scripture says about Him, just as we have accepted the many other promises written for our benefit.

When Jesus spoke to His disciples, He told them He was going away, but there was a Helper who would come and abide with them forever (see John 14:15). In other words this Helper was not restricted to an era of time, and His role was not to hurt the people of God but to help them. In fact, Jesus told us that Holy Spirit has many roles. One, He is a Helper (see John 14:26). Two, He will teach you all things (see John 14:26). Three, He will bring to our remembrance all things that Jesus said (see John 14:26). Four, He is to *"convict the world of sin, and of righteousness, and of judgment"* (John 16:8). And five, a.k.a. as the Spirit of truth, He will *"guide you into all truth...He will tell you things to come"* (John 16:13-14). With His many roles, the primary function He performs in our lives as it relates to prayer is the first one listed, He helps us.

If you have ever wanted to pray and have been unsure where to begin or what to say, Holy Spirit is the One who helps you by bringing to your remembrance what promise God has for your life based on Scripture. This attribute is wonderful to me because whenever I'm praying and I'm unsure what should be said next, it is Holy Spirit who brings to my attention what should be presented before God. With His help I can pray without consciously thinking about what I'm going to say next. He literally leads me from topic to topic immersed in God's will, regardless of the topics.

The second attribute of Holy Spirit that is very important to the believer as it relates to prayer is His intercession for us. There are times in life when we don't know what to pray, but there are also times when our loss for words are applicable to our own state of being. Either we're too drained, too upset, too confused, or just too overwhelmed by life that our prayers can feel empty. And when prayer feels empty, it makes it that much harder to begin. With the help of Holy Spirit, we can remove our intellect and allow our spirit to pray in our stead.

Romans 8:26-27 tells us *"the Spirit also helps in our weaknesses. For we do not know what we should pray for as we ought, but the Spirit Himself makes intercession for us with groanings which cannot be uttered. Now He who searches the hearts knows what the mind of the Spirit is, because He makes intercession for the saints according to the will of God."* You see, God knows those occasions when prayer is more than difficult, and in His great love for us, He provided a Helper. He's someone who helps us to pray, and He's also the One who will pray for us when we can't pray. The next time you wonder if there is anyone praying for you, I want you to be reminded that not only is Jesus making intercession for you (see Rom. 8:34), but Holy Spirit is also praying for you during the weakest points of your life.

The difference between Jesus praying for you and Holy Spirit is you play a role in Holy Spirit's intervention in your life. When Jesus prays, it's done in Heaven where we are not consciously aware of His prayers. When we pray with Holy Spirit, we open our mouths and intentionally speak with our spirit to God. *"For if I pray in a tongue, my spirit prays, but my understanding is unfruitful* (1 Cor. 14:14). *Meaning, "I will pray with the spirit, and I will also pray with the understanding"* (1 Cor. 14:15). We are obliged to pray in both manners but we cannot pray in tongues unless we invite Holy Spirit to speak through us and we're prepared to open our mouths and allow the utterance to flow.

What I mean is this. When John the Baptist baptized people, he used water for repentance, but when Jesus came to be baptized by John, the Holy Spirit descended like a dove, and Jesus became the

One who would baptize the believer in the Holy Spirit (see Mark 1:8). With this second baptism the believer would speak with new tongues. Just as we initiate ourselves to be water baptized, we must initiate ourselves to be baptized in Holy Spirit with the evidence of speaking in tongues.

Tongues should not frighten you as a believer because Scripture is not silent on tongues. The Book of Acts records the disciples, and the women who followed Jesus (and Mary, the mother of Jesus) were all in the upper room (see Acts 1:13-14) when *"there appeared to them divided tongues, as of fire, and one sat upon each of them. And they were all filled with the Holy Spirit and began to speak with other tongues, as the Spirit gave them utterance"* (Acts 2:3-4). Notice everyone in the upper room that day was baptized with Holy Spirit, and all who were baptized spoke in other tongues. You too can speak in other tongues as the Spirit gives you utterance. It is based on your desire to receive and your ability to believe that Holy Spirit is available to you just as He was available to those in the upper room that day. Jesus said in Luke 11:11, *"Which of you fathers, if your son asks for a fish, will give him a snake instead? Or if he asks for an egg, will give him a scorpion? If you then, though you are evil, know how to give good gifts to your children, how much more will your Father in heaven give the Holy Spirit to those who ask him!"* Holy Spirit is a good gift, and you can receive Him by simply asking our Father to give Him to you.

When you receive Holy Spirit, you should speak in other tongues, and then the benefit of His presence in your life can be realized in great measure. Not just because He's praying for you, but because He'll also begin to convict you and then strengthen you to judge the problem for correction (see John 16:8). And when you pray in the Spirit, Jude 20 says, you build yourself up in your most holy faith. Another benefit is that while you may not know what you're saying, Holy Spirit does, and He's praying the will of God in your life. Face it, we all want and need God's will in our lives, and if there is a way to communicate with God without getting in the way and in a manner that God will hear the sincerity of our hearts, we need to take advantage of that way.

We are encouraged to *"pray without ceasing"* in First Thessalonians 5:17. While praying with my understanding may be limited by where I am or what I'm doing, there is no limitation to praying in the Spirit.

Allow me to say this to you. There is no perfect way to receive Holy Spirit with the evidence of speaking in tongues. When I was baptized, I was with ladies who stood around me prodding me to say, "Hallelujah," "Glory," and anything else that would twist my tongue to speak. I was tarrying. I repeated everything they said, but it wasn't until I began to say from my own heart how much I loved the Lord and appreciated Him that I heard someone shout, "You did it!" Distracted by the shout, my tongues gave way to my own curiosity to hear myself. Once I focused on the Lord again, I spoke. And I have been speaking in tongues ever since. My husband's experience was quite private. He simply asked God for everything He read in the Bible and Holy Spirit filled him so he spoke while he knelt beside his bed. People wanting Holy Spirit are filled all the time as our team introduces who Holy Spirit is and how to receive Him with the evidence of speaking. Each time, people leave that room having been filled with Holy Spirit.

When we don't know how to pray or when we want to communicate with God without natural interference, we can allow our spirit to pray by opening our mouths and allowing the "utterance" of the Spirit to come forth (see Acts 2:4). When you begin to speak in other tongues, don't compare your tongues with another. Speak and allow Him time to pray for you sufficiently. I've heard of veterans in Christ who prayed in the Spirit for at least one hour daily, and they experienced great things in their lives and ministries. Each person attributed their success in life and ministry to the discipline they used to pray in the Spirit each day. Pursue Holy Spirit, and see God's purpose and plan for your life accelerated toward you.

A Personal Relationship

Isaiah 59:1 reads, *"Behold, the Lord's hand is not shortened, that it cannot save; nor His ear heavy, that it cannot hear. But your iniquities have separated you from your God; and your sins have hidden His face from you, so that He will not hear."* Jeremiah 5:25 says, *"Your iniquities have turned these things away, and your sins have withheld good from you."* Jeremiah 17:9-10 talks about the state of the heart. It reads, *"The heart is deceitful above all things, and desperately wicked; who can know it? I, the Lord search the heart, I test the mind, even to give every man according to his ways, according to the fruit of his doings."*

These Scriptures are harsh realities, and you may be wondering why I chose to place them in a book about prayer. I believe it is necessary to share these truths with you because if you are a person outside of relationship with the Lord (in other words, if you have never accepted Jesus Christ as your personal Savior and Lord), your prayers are hindered. Being found in Christ affords us the privileges and promises that I have written about thus far:

> *Therefore, brothers, since we have confidence to enter the Most Holy Place by the blood of Jesus, by a new and living way opened for us through the curtain, that is, His body, and since we have a great priest over the house of God, let us draw near to God with a sincere heart in full assurance of faith having our hearts sprinkled to cleanse us from a guilty conscience and having*

our bodies washed with pure water. Let us hold unswervingly to the hope we profess, for He who promised is faithful (Hebrews 10:19-23).

You'll find the Lord's Prayer and my personal testimony in the chapters that follow, but this working knowledge of how to communicate with God will mean nothing outside of relationship with Him.

Relationship with God doesn't require any work of your hand; it simply requires a heart of repentance, belief in Jesus Christ and His work for us, and a desire to have His leadership in your life. When relationship begins with God, we'll see our prayer lives really make a difference. When a relationship is ensued, unknowns become far less, and what is known becomes easier to accept and appreciate.

If you realize you do not have a personal relationship with Jesus, pray the words found in the back of this book from your heart and begin a beautiful, building relationship with our Father.

It is my prayer that you have enjoyed what you have read and that you will take the information to heart as you communicate with God. The second half of this book is designed to help you practice what you have read in theory. It is an exposé of the "Lord's Prayer" and serves as a guide that you may use to begin praying.

CHAPTER 13

GOD BLESS MOMMY; GOD BLESS DADDY

I remember the nights when I dutifully began to recite the Lord's Prayer, ending with "God bless Mommy, God bless Daddy, God bless Dwight [my brother], God bless Grandma in Durham, God bless Grandma in Charleston, God bless Grand-daddy, God bless Aunt Hallie, God bless Uncle Jack, God bless Aunt Anne, God bless, God bless, God bless, God bless…" The list went on and on until I drifted off to sleep. My job was done. This happened at the beginning of the week. The days that followed sounded like this: "God bless all those people I asked you to bless last night", and this, "God bless all those people from the other night," and this, "God bless all those people from the other-other night." When I felt too many days had passed, then I would say the litany again: The Lord's Prayer and God bless....

Prayer was important, but I didn't pray with understanding. Unfortunately, prayer is still misunderstood by many Christians. For most Christians, prayer is reserved for problems and needs. Often, it is an opportunity to beg God for something really important and then trust in a "stroke of luck" for results. Others understand that prayer is "talking to God," but they regard Him as mysterious and unpredictable. Then there are those Christians who are a little more seasoned in prayer, but make time with Him, seem mystical and reserved for those who are really, really holy. I have found out that prayer is for everyone, and God looks forward to mutual fellowship.

As a new Christian, I found my conversations with God were fulfilling, but in all honesty, they lasted about five minutes (and that was with effort). I wanted to talk to God, but I wanted prayer to be meaningful, not obligatory and superficial. Jesus asked the disciples why they couldn't pray or watch for just one hour (see Matt. 26:40). This hour mark became my goal. The trouble was that I didn't really have problems, so what was I going to pray? Well, I must say, being baptized in the Holy Spirit (with the evidence of speaking in tongues) was very helpful to me, because when I ran out of things to say to God, I just let my spirit speak.

Every time I prayed in the Spirit, it was as though God would show me who and what to pray for, and every time my prayers lasted at least one hour (without effort). I found myself praying God's written Word regarding situations or people. As I prayed in the Spirit, I was led to pray for people or issues I would never have considered naturally. It was during that time that I now believe God was birthing in me a heart of intercession.

Intercession meant I wasn't just talking to God about me, but I was talking to Him about issues regarding someone else. I was pleading with Him—using His Word—for grace and mercy toward another.

Remember when God sent angels to destroy Sodom and Gomorrah? (See Genesis 18:16-33.) It was Abraham who pleaded on behalf of the righteous. He knew the wrath of God was coming and intervened by asking God if He would destroy a city if fifty, then forty-five, finally ten righteous people lived there. Abraham acted as an intercessor for the righteous living in the midst of wickedness.

Jesus became our intercessor when God needed a mediator between Him and humankind. Hebrews 10:5-10 tells of Jesus' willingness to go in the likeness of man, for the sake of our relationship with God.

Ezekiel 22:30 also shows us the Lord's heart for intercession: *"So I sought for a man among them who would make a wall, and stand in the gap before Me on behalf of the land, that I should not destroy it; but found no one."* Without someone pleading the case of another, the wrath of God can be seen. But with someone who understands prayer, we can see the grace of God upon the lives of people. This is why understanding Jesus' teaching on prayer is so important. If there is no one who understands prayer, then there will be no one to stand in the gap for people.

Personally, there have been at least two occasions when I have known a group to be traveling by plane, and I sensed in my spirit they needed me to pray. I don't make myself out to be great, but I do make myself available, willing, and resolute enough to pray until I am released from the urgency. In each case, they have come home with reports of how terrible the flight was. In each case, I am confident that God heard my prayers, and His grace was sufficient for their lives.

I no longer have to pray the litany of God bless this one and that one. I can pray being led by the Spirit of God, using the Word of God, and having a confidence in God that He not only hears me, but He is willing to do what He promised (see 1 John 5:14-15). You, too, can pray the "Lord's Prayer" and see the hand of God in people or situations all around you.

A Pattern for Prayer

Many Christians get frustrated when their prayers appear to be unanswered; praying then seems to be futile. So rather than communicating more with God, we pray less, or we begin to pray more out of fear and unbelief than trust.

When my children were from two to five years old, they each went through the stage of meltdown when they didn't get what they wanted. All three of them at some point fell on the floor screaming at the top of their lungs. All three of them stood pulling on my pant leg begging for something. All three of them pouted about not having this or that. All three of them became mad at me as their mother because their assumptions were wrong. All three learned that these methods were futile. All three were told to stop whining and communicate; stop crying and talk; stop twirling on the floor and speak properly; stop and listen. In each case, they learned that Mommy doesn't respond to tantrums, so it was better to stop whining and get off of the floor if they really wanted results. They didn't say those words; they just adjusted their behavior.

Now honestly, there were times when I as a mother just gave in for the sake of peace. God doesn't just give in, however; He expects His children to grow in the principles that have been set from the beginning. To try to change God's way produces frustration. He is the same yesterday, today, and forever (see Heb. 13:8). He does not change (see Mal. 3:6). So how do we move the hand of God in our situations and life?

Jesus taught His disciples by giving the pattern to pray. As you consider the pattern for your personal application, please be clear that I am not telling you what to say. I am only giving a pattern or blueprint for prayer.

A pattern is just like the preparation an official would give you if you were going to speak to the President of the United States. You wouldn't be told what to say, but he or she would give you protocol on how issues should be broached. If you were traveling to another country, you wouldn't be told what to say, but you would be coached on that country's culture and code of ethics.

Allow me to present the pattern Jesus told us to use when we pray:

> *Our Father in heaven,*
> *Hallowed be Your name.*
> *Your kingdom come.*
> *Your will be done*
> *On earth as it is in heaven.*
> *Give us this day our daily bread.*
> *And forgive us our debts,*
> *As we forgive our debtors.*
> *And do not lead us into temptation,*
> *But deliver us from the evil one.*
> *For Yours is the kingdom and the power and*
> *The glory forever. Amen* (Matthew 6:9-13).

Praying these exact words may be commendable, but our goal should exceed piety and exemplify an earnest desire to build a fulfilling relationship with God. From this pattern to pray, we hold the key to the heart of God and the answers to being effective in His presence.

Father,
I pray Your children receive the pattern that You
have given for the sake of a rich fellowship with
You. Open the eyes of every person's
understanding concerning time with You so your
people come closer to You and You can become
closer to them.
In Jesus' name. Amen.

For results in prayer, recognize God reveals Himself and His desires so that we may pursue Him effectively.

CHAPTER 14

OUR FATHER IN HEAVEN

One of the most interesting things that Jesus says to the disciples about prayer is how to begin. Throughout the Old Testament or the Old Covenant, the people addressed God as God. He was often called the "God of Abraham, the God of Isaac, and the God of Jacob," and He referred to Himself by that title as well. The enemies of Israel referred to Him as the "God of Israel." Nebuchadnezzar, the king of Babylon, called Him the Holy God.

The people and the kings of Israel feared God. This fear was more than reverence; it was trepidation: *"Then they said to Moses, 'You speak with us, and we will hear; but let not God speak with us, lest we die'"* (Exod. 20:19). Israel only knew God's hand, His authority, and power. Few knew God beyond His power to provide.

Abraham, Moses, David, and Enoch are examples of the few men of that time who had a developed relationship with God. Even so, none of these men besides David referred to Him as Father. In Psalm 68:5, David said, God is a *"father of the fatherless."* His reference to God as Father wasn't personal, however, because he still addressed God as Lord.

The prophet Isaiah prophesied God as our Father in Isaiah 9:6. *"For unto us a Child is born, unto us a Son is given; and the government will be upon His shoulder. And His name will be called Wonderful, Counselor, Mighty God, Everlasting Father, Prince of Peace."*

The prophetic word in Isaiah is our reality today. Jesus taught the disciples how to pray by telling them to pray, "Our *Father* in heaven." In other words, no longer is it necessary to consider God in His authority alone, but as children of God, you may call Him your Father. He's no longer just the one you have access to because of His power; through Jesus, you may approach Him unguarded, with confidence and assuredness.

Our ability to call God "Father" exemplifies a relationship with God that is no longer legalistic, formal, or filled with apprehension. Paul said, *"you did not receive the spirit of bondage again to fear* [this word *fear* in the Greek means, "alarm or fright"; to be afraid, exceedingly, fear, terror], *but you received the Spirit of adoption by whom we cry out, 'Abba Father.' The Spirit Himself bears witness with our spirit that we are children of God, and if children, then heirs—heirs of God and joint heirs with Christ, if indeed we suffer with Him, that we may also be glorified together"* (Rom. 8:14-17).[1] The Israelites didn't have the opportunity that we have to address God as Father. The law was given, but it didn't allow the confidence needed to develop such a bond. Think about it, tradition states that the priest went in with the sacrifices for the people's sins wearing a rope that was used to drag his dead body out of the Holy of holies if he didn't enter God's presence properly. This level of fear should not be part of healthy father-child relationships. This kind of fear brought a high regard for God's authority but limited the freedom and desire to pursue intimate relationship.

Thank God for Jesus! Fear doesn't have to be our testimony. Jesus came so that our access to "His" Father enables us to address God just like He did, "Father." Therefore our prayers shouldn't consistently address God in title alone: "And God," "O God," "Thank You, God," "I love You, God..." That's like a child referring to her daddy as "Mr. Smith"—or the family calling the daddy of the house "Head of the household": "Oh, and Head of the household, Mr. Smith...."

It is true that our actions, not our address alone, speak to how much we respect God. However, our prayer life should be intimate enough to allow us to address our God as Father. Our prayer life is where a conversation with the Creator of all can ensue. Prayer is a time of vulnerability when every façade is removed for the purpose of meaningful interaction. During this time of talking to God, we grow toward seeing Him as our Father, the One who gives safety, the One we can trust, the One who protects and provides, and the One who gives us confidence in knowing we can come to Him anytime. He's always available, always reachable, and those who seek Him will never lack for anything good (see Ps. 34:10).

The God of the Old Covenant is the Father of the New Covenant. Because He is our Father, we can come to Him knowing that He may chastise us, He may give us boundaries, but His desire for us is only good. Therefore we can come to Him recognizing a couple of things.

First, we don't have to be timid; Hebrews 4:16 says we can come boldly to His throne to obtain mercy and find grace. All because

Jesus, our Big Brother, made a way for all who desire to enter in through the shed blood of Christ.

Second, if we continue to come to Him even in our mistakes and shortcomings, Jesus can continue to represent us and identify us as holy, blameless, and above reproach. Colossians 1:21-23 tells us that "[we], *who once were alienated and enemies in* [our] *mind by wicked works, yet now He has reconciled in the body of His flesh through death, to present* [us] *holy, and blameless, and above reproach in His sight—if indeed* [we] *continue in the faith, grounded and steadfast, and are not moved away from the hope of the gospel which* [we] *heard, which was preached to every creature under heaven."* It's the "if" that determines our spiritual state; even when we have made mistakes, we do not fail *if* we "continue in the faith."

As an example, we can consider Peter and Judas. Both men made a terrible mistake. Peter denied Jesus, and Judas betrayed Him. Both men wept bitterly with great remorse, yet one man despaired and hanged himself (see Matt. 27:5). The other, with penance, lived, and an angel was able to say in Mark 16:7, *"go, tell His disciples—and Peter…"* These men sinned, but only one continued. Peter could have decided the guilt was unbearable just as Judas did. Peter could have been so condemned that when they came to get him, along with the disciples, his sense of unworthiness could have proved to be greater than his hope for forgiveness. Peter could have quit, but he decided to accept forgiveness and continue.

When you know you're talking to your Father who loves you, you know you can always come back. You recognize you have a relationship that may have become tenuous, but it's never over unless you consciously decide to end it.

In this pattern we should begin our conversation with God, knowing that He is our Father; He does love us, and He's always available because our Big Brother made it possible. He's not just

God, but He's a Father who cares enough to open the door for our complete access to Him through His Son Jesus Christ.

> *If we confess our sins, He is faithful and just to forgive our sins and to cleanse us from all unrighteousness* (1 John 1:9).

> *My Father,*
> *You who are in Heaven: Thank You for Your Spirit that bears witness with my spirit that I am Your child and that I am an heir together with Christ Jesus* (see Rom. 8:14-17). *May Christ be in me, and my witness always be authentic and sincere as I come boldly to Your throne to obtain mercy and find grace in every area of my life* (see Heb. 4:16). *I acknowledge You as my God and my Father. May I always be the apple of Your eye* (see Ps. 17:8), *and may I always recognize You as my Rock and Salvation*
> (see Ps. 62:2,6-7).

For results in prayer, recognize that you must have a relationship with God through Jesus Christ.

Endnote

1. See http://biblelexicon.org/romans/8-15.htm; "phobos."

CHAPTER 15

HALLOWED BE YOUR NAME

Just after our declaration of God as our Father, Jesus tells us to describe His Name as hallowed. *Hallowed* means "holy," and *holy* means "to set apart." *Holy* is also defined as that which is sacred, and *sacred* means "worthy of worship." Thus, we are not constrained to say, *"Hallowed be Your Name"* alone. No! These words give the children of God a pattern for praising God in His sovereignty.

If we use these words as a pattern, then prayer becomes encouraging to us personally, magnifying God above every situation, problem, or person. It's in worship that we focus not on the problem, but on the solution, almighty God. Jesus is saying to the disciples, when you pray, acknowledge your Father by *saying who He is*.

The Book of Matthew recounts many great examples of those following this pattern of prayer through worship.

In Matthew 8:2, a leper *"worshiped Him, saying, 'Lord, if You are willing, You can make me clean.'"* He's essentially saying, "I know that You're able to make me clean. I have no doubt in my mind or heart that's why I'm before You with this problem. Yet, I'm not giving glory to the problem by announcing it; I'm giving glory to You by acknowledging Your dominion over it and Your ability to remove it from my life—that is, if You're willing." In this leper's declaration, Jesus is hallowed.

In Matthew 9:18, a ruler came to Jesus because his daughter died. The Scripture says this ruler *"worshiped Him saying, 'my daughter has just died, but come and lay Your hand on her and she will live.'"* This ruler approached Jesus with confidence in His ability to raise up his dead child. His confidence in Jesus' ability gave him words that are defined as worship.

Notice the words of worship are spoken without doubt or hesitation, and they express trust in the ability of Christ. There was no begging in either example. Only truth came out of the leper's and the ruler's mouth. When you pray, what comes out of your mouth? Are you worshiping God through a declaration of His ability, or are you questioning His power? Trusting in truth is defined as worship. Trusting in facts (information received as truth based on senses: hearing, tasting, touching, smelling and in Thomas' case, seeing) is defined as unbelief. If we look at the interaction between Jesus and Thomas in John 20:24-29, Jesus reproves Thomas for needing facts (*"Unless I see in His hands the print of the nails, and put my hand into His side, I will not believe."*) in order to believe. After meeting Thomas's criteria to believe, Jesus tells him, *"Do not be unbelieving, but believing"* (John 20:27). Hebrews 3:12 goes so far to say, *"Beware, brethren, lest there be in any of you an evil heart of unbelief in departing from the living God."*

When you pray worshiping God, you are acknowledging and accepting His power over every fact represented in your life. Don't let facts overshadow the truth in your life. Let God's truth take precedence by your conscious decision to worship Him in spirit and in truth! (see John 4:23).

Another example of worship is the Canaanite woman's desperate plea to get help for her daughter. She wasn't even a Hebrew woman, yet she came assured that this Jesus had the ability to help her. She didn't tell Jesus how she might not qualify. She didn't make Jesus a bunch of promises she knew she wouldn't keep. She simply came acknowledging who Jesus was and His ability. Matthew 15:25 says, *"she came and worshiped Him, saying, 'Lord, help me!'"* She didn't ask if He could help her. She knew He had the ability to help her, and she was intent on getting His help that day.

You see when we worship God, we are declaring His ability and authority; we are acknowledging Him as the answer for every situation or problem life has presented.

To pursue the pattern in "Hallowed be Your Name," we worship. We declare God as *Jehovah-Jireh*, our Provision, when our lack confronts us (see Gen. 22:14). We declare God as *Jehovah-Tsidkenu*, our Righteousness, when, as believers, our wrong decisions condemn us (see Jer. 23:5-8). We declare God as *Jehovah-Rapha*, our Physician, when doctors have given their own perspective (see Exod. 15:22-26). To declare who God is in the midst of situations is to worship God. Thus, "Hallowed be Thy name!"

It's a time to acquiesce to the power and ability of God—whether you are in plenty or in need. In each biblical scenario, these people had a real need. They came to Jesus with intention, acknowledged His ability to handle the situation, and He received their request based on their worship.

Their worship wasn't politically correct; they worshiped with desperation and determination. Their approach wasn't timid; they approached with confidence. Their knowledge of Jesus didn't limit their resolve; they came without hesitation and without concern for the opinions of others. They came declaring who He was and what He could do.

Likewise, your approach to our Father is not contingent upon how well versed you are theologically, or how long you have attended church, or how insignificant your situation may seem to another. Your answer from God is based on your decision to worship Him relentlessly rather than bemoan the situation every time you're before Him.

This part of the Lord's Prayer should not be taken for granted or taken lightly. When turmoil surrounds us, we worship out of our confidence in His ability to help. Because we know God as our Father, we can worship and see His hand move in our lives.

Every moment of the day you have the opportunity to say, "Hallowed be Your name," Father. You don't have to wait for Sunday. Let's face it, problems don't wait for Sunday; thus, your solution doesn't have to wait either. You don't have to wait for the perfect person with the perfect title to pray. You have the opportunity to worship Him now: "Your name is Holy;" "Nothing is too hard for You, Father;" "You are good;" "Your name is above every name;" "Your name is high and lifted up." It's in His Name that victory is received in your life.

Even Jesus worshiped when raising Lazarus from the dead. He said, in John 11:41-43, *"'Father, I thank You that You have heard Me* [worship]. *And I know that You always hear Me* [worship], *but because of the people who are standing by I said this, that they may believe that You sent Me.' Now when He had said these things, He cried with a loud voice, 'Lazarus, come forth!'"*

126

Jesus acknowledged God's ability to hear. He acknowledged that God always heard Him. "Hallowed be thy name" is to acknowledge with confidence who He is and what He is able to do in your life, your situation, your family, your heart.

Worship God beyond the four words, "Hallowed Be Thy Name," and consider the pattern.

> *My Father,*
> *I worship You for You are Holy, and*
> *You reign in my life:*
> *For there is no one like unto You, Abba (see Rom.*
> *8:15). You are the strength of my life;*
> *You are my song (see Ps. 118:14), and my hiding*
> *place (see Ps. 32:7). For You are my sun and my*
> *shield; You give grace and glory. No good thing*
> *will You withhold from me (see Ps. 84:11). You*
> *are a very present help in this time of trouble (see*
> *Ps. 46:1). You are my glory and the lifter of my*
> *head (see Ps. 3:3). You are my light and my*
> *salvation (see Ps. 27:1). You are the joy of my life.*
> *You, Father, are the reason I live.*
> *In Jesus' name I pray, Lord. Amen.*

For results, don't take this aspect of prayer for granted. *Holy* means "sacred," and *sacred* means "worthy of worship."

CHAPTER 16

YOUR KINGDOM COME

If we want results when we pray, we must understand that God's ways are not like our ways. We are mortal, trying to understand the immortal, invisible, and all-knowing God.

I remember visiting a church, and during the service a prophetic word came forth. In the word, the direction was to "run." Obviously, I don't know everything, but my understanding of the word *run* was different from others. I heard the word *run* and began to consider my pursuit of purpose. There were other people who heard the word *run* and began to literally run! Running fast, they swirled around the sanctuary one after the other. Their actions surprised me, and I wondered if it would make a difference in their lives. Either way, our interpretations were different.

My point is that truth can be misinterpreted. Regardless of who was wrong or right in my example, we either went away fulfilled, or one (or both) of us missed an opportunity to consider the truth with proper application.

Jesus spoke truth to both the crowds and His disciples. He spoke using parables, but Scripture shows several occasions when even the disciples did not understand what Jesus was saying. When they didn't understand, the disciples had the opportunity to inquire more. In each case, Jesus explained the meaning of the stories and their proper application to God's children. Even more, when we don't understand but earnestly desire understanding, God will reveal the meaning behind what we read too. Psalm 25:14 says, *"The secret of the Lord is with those who fear Him, and He will show them His covenant."*

Thus, I believe God has given me understanding of the pattern set before us in this portion of the Lord's Prayer, "Your Kingdom Come." I don't presume to have the complete revelation, but I believe God has revealed this truth to me so that we can all benefit in our understanding of God's kingdom coming in our midst.

When Jesus came, the people thought He should be made King of Israel in the natural. Here was a man who fed the multitude, spoke with authority, knew the Law, healed those brought to Him, and did many other wonderful things. This man was worthy enough to be the King of Israel. He was the one they anxiously waited for to deliver them from bondage and the oppression of Rome. They assumed His Kingdom was like the kingdoms of the world. Jesus, knowing their heart and His purpose, would always leave before they could declare Him king (see John 6:15). You see, the people misunderstood truth. Jesus didn't come to sit on a man-made throne; He came to establish His Kingdom in our hearts. Thus, Jesus said in Luke 17:21, *"...the kingdom of God is within you."*

In another example, Pilate asked Jesus if He was the king of the Jews, supposing His rule was of the earth. Jesus replied, *"My kingdom is not of this world. If My kingdom were of this world, My servants would fight, so that I should not be delivered to the Jews"* (John 18:36). Pilate, too, didn't understand Jesus' position.

Even the disciples were concerned about God's special people being subject to another. They wondered when Israel would have rule again. In Acts 1:6 they asked, *"Lord, are You at this time going to restore the kingdom to Israel?"* (NIV). They were looking for a physical kingdom because they were limited in understanding.

These examples show us how shortsighted we can be, and how our limited understanding can lead to ineffectiveness. So, what is Jesus saying in this day when He counsels us to pray, *"Your Kingdom Come"*?

Seeking the Kingdom

Too often we focus on ourselves when we pray, and we rarely consider God's will in general. This misunderstanding in prayer can leave us without answers because our motives are so self-centered. James 4:1-3 talks about not receiving from God because we ask God amiss. The next sentence defines how we err: *"you ask with wrong motives, that you may spend* [it] *on your pleasures"* (NIV).

I don't believe God is against His children having things, but I do believe He expects us to *"seek first the kingdom of God and His righteousness"* (Matt. 6:33). Then, as the verse continues, *"all these things shall be added to* [us]*"* (Matt. 6:33). Let me repeat, we're to seek the Kingdom of God.

James 4:4 gives us further insight on how our prayers become amiss. It reads, *"Adulterers and adulteresses! Do you not know that friendship with the world is enmity with God? Whoever therefore wants to be a friend of the world makes himself an enemy of God."* Our motivation in prayer must be based on God's will for our lives which is found in His Kingdom and in His righteousness. His greatest desire is that His children walk in relationship with Him, and this relationship is developed through our obedience to His Word (see Deut. 11:1; Dan. 9:4; John 14:15,21,23-24). When we walk according to His Word, we're living by the standards of the Kingdom. When we walk contrary to His will, we show ourselves as lovers of the world, committing spiritual adultery and making ourselves God's enemy. Obviously, no enemy of God can expect to receive from God. In fact, if we look at Israel's example of this same sin (spiritual adultery), we see a people punished after many warnings—Hosea, Jeremiah, Isaiah, Ezekiel were just a few of the prophets who warned the people about spiritual harlotry—and in the end crying out to God for deliverance.

Unfortunately our society embraces the same sin through compromises, which in the end hinder and prevent answers to prayer.

Thus, to pray *"Your Kingdom Come"* is to receive His authority, rule, and leadership in our personal lives and in the earth.

The world does not yield to the Kingdom of God. First John 2:15 says, *"Do not love the world or the things in the world. If anyone loves the world, the love of the Father is not in him."* As Christians, we easily receive Christ as our Savior, but we resist His Lordship in our lives. Yet, in the Kingdom of God, Jesus Christ must be Savior and Lord. Not one or the other, but both.

For Jesus to be Lord, a choice must be made to invite the Kingdom of God into our lives. Thus, we're yielding our rights to God and His authority. We're giving up our will, our plans, and our decisions to God's leadership. In return, we can expect to be provided for, cared for, and protected. With Christ as King, we are established and we are affirmed.

Monarchies are not completely foreign to most of us. We read about it in Scripture as kings dispose of nations, set up rule, and declare laws. We look at television programs that depict kings with absolute authority. Yet when we talk about the Kingdom in our personal lives, we balk because our culture celebrates independence, fights for freedom, and only tolerates submission. Romans 6:18-20 tells us, however, that Christ set us free from slavery to sin so that we can now *offer the parts of* [our] *body...in slavery to righteousness* (NIV). You and I will obey something. When you pray the Kingdom, you're praying God's whole agenda for the heart of man and on earth. We're praying God's Lordship in totality.

When we're praying "the Kingdom" for ourselves, we're praying that we understand who we are in Christ Jesus so that excuses can no longer keep us from obedience. As Christians, we need His power demonstrated in our weaknesses, His authority expressed over our timidity, His love seen above our selfishness. If we don't pray the established Kingdom of God in our lives, we'll be fruitless in our efforts to serve the Lord.

When we're praying "the Kingdom" in the lives of other people, we're asking God to intervene in the lives of men and women who will follow the dictates of their own evil hearts without His presence (see Jer. 7:24). Obedience and surrender is not possible without the Father's intervention; that's why Jesus said, "Pray." Pray not just these words, "Thy Kingdom Come," but by the grace of God pray for truth to triumph over deception, for His standard to be raised up in the earth. Pray for obedience. Pray that people would repent and turn away from a heart of unbelief. Pray for His will, His authority, His plans, His purposes, and His love to be realized. Ask God to show Himself to a people who continually turn their backs on Him. By praying the Kingdom, we're asking God to put in us a standard of righteousness that steers our course of life toward His glory, honor, and praise.

Virtually every day I leave my home and interact with one person or another. I have the opportunity to talk about the weather, talk about the game, talk about the news or even mention the latest multi-level marketing opportunity. Not only do I have this opportunity to speak to people, but Christians like me, everywhere, have this opportunity. Yet we rarely use our opportunity to talk to strangers about the Gospel of Jesus Christ. We may tell where we go to church or share what event is happening in our church, but oddly, we're hesitant when it comes to the gospel. When we pray the kingdom it's this hesitancy that we break. Personally, when I pray the kingdom of God in the earth, I'm become very alert to those around me and their need of salvation. No longer do I prioritize other topics, and no longer have I shifted the responsibility to win the lost on someone else, including God. When I pray the kingdom in the earth I recognize it is my duty to win the lost; therefore, I along with other Christians, need the boldness and the concern that pushes beyond comfort levels and into complete obedience. Jesus said, "The harvest truly is plentiful, but the laborers are few. Therefore pray the Lord of the harvest to send out laborers into His harvest" (Matt. 9:37-39). If we're praying for laborers, we will be a little more sensitive to our role as it relates to seeing the Kingdom of God come here in the earth. Praying the Kingdom can then make a difference all around us. And God is pleased.

Second Chronicles 7:14 says, *"If My people, who are called by My name, will humble themselves and pray and seek My face and turn from their wicked ways, then I will hear from heaven and will forgive their sin and will heal their land"* (NIV). Three men who saw the natural and spiritual state of their nation obeyed and are now biblical testaments to the power of prayer. Nehemiah (see Neh. 1), King Josiah (see 2 Kings 22,23), and Daniel (see Dan. 9) humbled themselves and set their hearts to see the glory of the Kingdom of God restored. God honored their commitment.

Who said that our prayers, as believers, don't mean anything?

When we pray God's Kingdom, we are willing to humble ourselves before God's throne and to stand in the gap for people to know Him. If everyone follows the pattern presented by Jesus, we'll see revival spark and penetrate the land. We'll be like John the Baptist, saying, "The Kingdom of God (His will, His power, His dominion, His love, His greatness, His sovereignty, His authority, His plan, His purpose, His rule, His majesty, His royalty) has come near you: *'Repent and believe the good news!'*" (see Mark 1:15 NIV).

When we gear our prayers to the larger picture, our rewards will far outweigh what the world has to offer.

Father,
It is Your presence in my life that I so desire and
need. I love You and appreciate You, but more
than anything, I need You. Reveal Yourself to me
according to Your loving-kindness, according to
Your multiple mercies. Your presence in my life is
what I long for. May Your Kingdom be established
in me so it's no longer my way, my will, and my
plan. You are the Sovereign King, and I yield to
Your leadership. May I be a vessel of honor,
sanctified unto You and prepared for every good
work (see 2 Tim. 2:21). May my life be a sweet
savor unto You. May I be used by You to see the
Kingdom expanded.
Today, I yield myself to speak to people
concerning the cross of Christ (see Rom. 1:16).

*May I live with a conviction to see Your Kingdom
expanded in the earth today (see Matt. 9:38). I
desire the conviction of the Holy Spirit. Fulfill
Your plan in the earth, and let Your will be done,
Your authority be recognized, and Your Lordship
made preeminent.
May my heart be ever yielding to You in purpose
and position. May my life mirror Christ (see*
Eph. 5:1) *in obedience and with fruits of righteousness*
(see Phil. 1:11) *May my life in You go beyond talk
so Your Kingdom may be established in power*
(see 1 Cor. 4:20).
In Jesus' name. Amen.

For results in prayer, understand God's ways are different from
your ways and be ever yielding to His ways.

CHAPTER 17

YOUR WILL BE DONE ON EARTH AS IT IS IN HEAVEN

Now that we are in the presence of our Father and have worshiped, consecrated our lives, and prayed for the salvation of humankind, it would seem that it is time to make requests of God. The key, however, is to know the will of God.

We know God's will is accomplished in Heaven (see Matt. 6:10). Now we can use the pattern to pray His will in the earth (in our country, state, city, families, lives, future, etc.). First John 5:14 says, *"Now this is the confidence that we have in Him, that if we ask anything according to His will, He hears us. And if we know that He*

TEACH ME TO PRAY

hears us, whatever we ask, we know we have the petitions that we have asked of him." This promise is good news because we have guaranteed answers if we pray His will. God's will is not hidden, but it is made available in His Word to all of us.

The challenge is to study His Word so we pray with knowledge and not with religious jargon. For example, God doesn't want any to perish, according to Second Peter 3:9, so we can pray with confidence concerning our loved ones. God's will is that a man would love his wife like Christ loved the Church (see Eph. 5:25 NIV), so we can confidently pray for a giving husband. When we need joy and peace, it's God's will—as seen in Romans 15:13. These and many other Scriptures are available for application in our prayer lives. We don't have to concoct anything. We just need to know God's will from His Word, believe it, and expect it.

Matthew 6:33 tells us how to ask for basic necessities: *"Seek first the kingdom of God and His righteousness, and all these things shall be added to you."* In modern-day Christianity, however, many of us have reversed the order. We bend our knees to ask God for stuff and call that building relationship. While I understand the temptation to do this (because I've been guilty), I must present a caution.

David compares Moses' and Israel's relationship with God in Psalm 103:7: *"He made known His ways to Moses, His acts to the children of Israel."* Let's examine Israel's relationship with God first. Historically, Israel rarely called on God for fellowship. They called on Him when they were losing a war, afraid of an enemy, oppressed by a situation, when they wanted meat or needed water.

They rejoiced in God when they experienced victory and forgot about God when the problem was over and the celebration ended. Their relationship with God was legalistic. Their hearts were removed from God because they didn't know Him beyond law.

This mindset followed Israel into the New Testament as Jesus exposed their motives saying, *"I tell you the truth, you are looking for me, not because you saw miraculous signs but because you ate the loaves and had your fill"* (John 6:26). The Pharisees sought after Jesus too, but only to catch him in something He might say. (Luke 11:53-54 NIV). Our motives are important to God.

Moses was different. God actually made known His ways to him. To know someone's ways is to be familiar with what he or she does and have understanding of why that person does it. The Hebrew dictionary defines *ways* in Psalm 103:7 as "road," "journey," "habit," or "manner."[1] In other words, God didn't just go through the guidelines with Moses; He talked with Moses and fellowshipped with him. As Christians, our aim should be to know the ways of God, not just His provision. When we fellowship to know Him, those things come automatically: *"His divine power has given us everything we need for life and godliness through our knowledge of Him who called us by His own glory and goodness"* (2 Pet. 1:3 NIV).

Praying God's Will

So how do we pray, *"Your will be done on earth as it is in heaven"*? If we look at Scripture, we see how everything in Heaven shows sincere reverence and honor for God. Everything and every being has purpose through Him, in Him, and for Him. The will of our Father in Heaven centers around Him alone. Angels are not the center of attention, but God is. Created things are not the center of attention; God is. Everything acknowledges God with reverence. All worship, adoration, thanksgiving, and glory is given to God. To be in the presence of God is an opportunity to know Him in His greatness, love, compassion, and kindness. So rather than look to those things we ask and need from God as a source of joy, we have the promise in having the fullness of joy by simply being in His presence (see Ps. 16:11).

When we pray, we must be careful not to center each time of fellowship with Him on the problem, uncertainty, or care we have in life. There ought to be time in prayer designated for fellowship alone. No one likes a user; we'd rather be confident that a friend stands by us out of genuine caring. Nevertheless, petitions made by those in relationship with God are different from petitions made by those who neither have nor desire true relationship.

Just as in days of old, some of us come to God in relationship with Him, and others come just wanting something from Him. God is gracious, but what we receive is based on the integrity of our heart: *"I, the Lord, search the heart, I test the mind, even to give every man according to his ways, according to the fruit of his doings"* (Jer. 17:10). For there is no good thing that God withholds from them whose walk is blameless (see Ps. 84:11 NIV).

If you recognize that your motivation to pray was based on God's hand alone, you can change. To be convicted of wrong behavior doesn't mean we have to give up on change. Holy Spirit convicts us of sin in order to provoke change, not create hopelessness.

Become transparent before God even now. Prayer is being honest with who you are and what you're thinking regardless of how shameful you may feel it to be. When we acknowledge our shortcomings, God is always ready to step in and be our Father and friend. He's close to the contrite (repentant, regretful, sorry): *"Has not My hand made all these things, and so they came into being?' declares the Lord. 'This is the one I esteem: he who is humble and contrite in spirit, and trembles at My word'"* (Isa. 66:2 NIV).

In prayer we should be truly vulnerable and honest with our thoughts, issues, cares, problems, etc. You cannot trick, manipulate, or fool God. God is completely aware of our motives. Think about it, satan was thrown out of Heaven, not because of something he said aloud or because of outward rebellion, but because of what he said in his heart (see Isa. 14:13). Our heart holds our motives. Thus we'll either see our request manifest (in God's timing), or we'll languish waiting for answers to our requests.

Don't frustrate yourself. Pursue God with a pure heart. Desire Him, not His hands. In doing so, you'll find your prayer life to be that much more rewarding.

When you pursue Him in reverence, His promise in Psalm 33:18-19 becomes His will for your life: *"But the eyes of the Lord are on those who fear Him, on those whose hope is in His unfailing love, to deliver them from death and keep them alive in famine"* (NIV). Death is anything that drains life from you, and famine is anything that looks barren in your life. Our God is there for those who look to and rest in His love.

Our prayers don't have to be filled with tears of uncertainty. Neither do our prayers have to fluctuate between praise and expressions of doubt. We don't have to beg, and we don't have to fall apart: *"God is not a man, that He should lie, nor a son of man, that He should change His mind. Does He speak and then not act? Does He promise and not fulfill?"* (Num. 23:19 NIV). It's in these promises that we can be strengthened in our resolve to trust and hope in our God.

When David and his troops returned to Ziklag in First Samuel 30, they found the city burned and their relatives abducted. The Bible says three things happened: David and the people cried until they could cry no more, then David became distressed because the people were prepared to stone him and finally, David strengthened himself in the Lord. First Samuel 30:7 reads, *"Then David said to Abiathar the priest, Ahimelech's son, 'Please bring the ephod here to me.'"* And Abiathar brought the ephod to David. So David inquired of the Lord, saying, "Shall I pursue this troop? Shall I overtake them?" God gave David an answer and God will give you an answer too. After you have cried until you can cry no more and after you have allowed worry to steal your sleep one last time, strengthen yourself in the Lord by seeking God's face. The same God that directed David will direct you.

Maybe you're experiencing specific needs. God's will is for every need to be supplied. Find your answer in the Word of God, pray the promise, and see the change. Maybe you don't have a need, just plenty of desires. The same is true. Find the promise, pray the promise, and know God hears you: *"For all the promises of God in Him are Yes, and in Him Amen"* (2 Cor. 1:20). The promises of God are all *yes* in Christ Jesus. It is the Father's pleasure to give us good things.

Father,
Your will is that everything with breath would
praise You (see Ps. 150:6). I purpose to praise You
like the Heavenly Host. I declare You are the One
who is, and the One who was, and the One who is
to come (see Rev. 16:5). You are Righteous in
Your Being. There is none like You. Your throne O
God is forever and ever. "A scepter of
righteousness is the scepter of Your Kingdom"
(Ps. 45:6). I gladly bow before You, for You are
holy, righteous, and good. "Amen! Blessing and
glory and wisdom, thanksgiving and honor and
power and might" be Yours forever and ever
(Rev. 7:12).
As Your glory is seen in the heavens, let Your
glory be seen in the earth and in my life. Through
all that I do and say, I seek after You, Abba. Thank

You for food (see Matt. 6:25-33), *peace* (see Isa.
26:3), *promotion* (see Ps. 75:6-7), *vindication* (see
Ps. 17:2), *protection* (see Ps. 91:11-12), *liberty,
healing, and comfort* (see Isa. 61:1,3), *and my new
_____ [fill in the blank]* (see Ps. 37:4).
*Thank You for complete provision and blessing
Father.
In Jesus' Name. Amen.*

For results in this prayer, we must recognize all things come
from God and He takes care of His children. God is not
slack concerning His promises.

Endnote

1. *Strong's Exhaustive Concordance.* Nelson. Hebrew and
Chaldee Dictionary, Number 1870 ,

CHAPTER 18

GIVE US THIS DAY OUR DAILY BREAD

If we're not careful, we'll get this part of prayer confused with the pattern shown in *"Your will be done on earth as it is in heaven."* Both involve knowing the Word of God as our source of truth for prayer. However, the previous stanza is based on knowledge of the will of God and addresses specific needs in our lives that require answers. In this portion, *"Give us today our daily bread,"* the Word of God is our Daily Bread and must be consumed, not just known.

If we're to pray according to pattern, we must identify the bread we are asking our Father to give.

Bread is referenced as a necessity in our lives in two places. When God lead Israel out of Egypt, He wanted them to understand they

145

would no longer live by the bread they were accustomed to alone, but now they would live by the very words of God (see Deut. 8:3). This lesson was so important to God that He tested them by causing them to hunger. It was a difficult test for Israel as they learned how to trust God as their source instead of what they had known in Egypt. So when they wanted and needed food, God provided the manna and/or quail, but His ultimate desire was for the people to trust His Word, His voice, and His direction. His very Word was Israel's bread just as Jesus, who is the Word come in flesh (see John 1:14), is the bread of life to the Christian today.

Now in the New Testament Jesus teaches the believer the same principle of trust posed in parable form. Matthew 6:25-26 says, *"Therefore I tell you, do not worry about your life, what you will eat or drink; or about your body, what you will wear....Look at the birds of the air; they do not sow or reap or store away in barns, and yet your heavenly Father feeds them. Are you not much more valuable than they?"* (NIV). If we're compared to a bird, we should be confident that our worth is much greater; thus our expectation should be, God will provide food for our table. If we worry about His provision, then we are like the Gentiles who have no promise of provision (see Matt. 6:32). To underscore His provision, Jesus showed how easy it was to feed people food when He multiplied the fish and the loaves (see John 6). Even Isaiah said in Psalm 37:25, *"I have never seen the righteous forsaken or their children begging bread"* (NIV).

God provides bread to eat, thus asking for this kind of bread is not necessary. Yet bread defined as the Word of God is something that we need daily. One reason is because we need His Word to help people, spiritually. When Jesus spoke truth to the Samaritan woman in John 4, his disciples arrived with food wanting Him to eat, but Jesus said, "I have food to eat that you know nothing about." To offer clarity he says, *"My food is to do the will of Him who sent me and to finish His work"* (John 4:34). He then tells us to pray for laborers in a harvest that's ripe for salvation.

When we pray, *"Give us today our daily bread,"* we ask God to lead us in His will for the day. As seen with Jesus, His will includes our ministry to other people. It doesn't mean we all have to change our profession to pastor or evangelist, but it should be our desire to be used of God in the day. On one occasion it may mean giving someone a word of encouragement, on another it may mean giving the Gospel to a lost person, and then on another occasion it may mean giving money to someone or to some cause. When we live our lives daily in obedience to God, we are just as fulfilled as Jesus was on the day the woman at the well received the bread of life.

Moreover, every day we go into a world filled with contradictions. Every day, the world offers lust, pride, and more lust (see 1 John 2:16). Every day, the Christian must be equipped to stand. Most of us don't walk around with a Bible in tow, so the Word must be in our hearts. The Word must be so available in our hearts that no matter what the opposition, the Word becomes the sword to fight and the solution to life.

When we pray *"Give us today our daily bread,"* we're asking God to equip us with His Word for that day. Only God knows what is in front of us, and only God's Word can make the difference in how we process truth and obtain ultimate victory or defeat. Psalm 119:11 reads, *"I have hidden Your word in my heart, that I might not sin against you"* (NIV).

What's in your heart is revealed when you stub your baby toe, become stuck in traffic, or are forced to apologize to a difficult person. Your response to any of those experiences clues you in on the amount of bread you have eaten, stored, or skipped. Our response to those unplanned moments helps us to see what's really in our hearts and should convict us to pursue His Word more diligently, or make us appreciate the time we've used to write the Word of God on the tablet of our heart (see Prov. 7:2-3). These are small incidents that happen in life, but there are harder situations that can knock the wind out of the strongest Christian: the untimely death of a loved one, the unexpected loss of a job, the shameless behavior of a child, or the sadness of unmet goals. These too come in life and prove the genuineness of professed faith. We need the daily Word of God so we may withstand any storm.

Being Prepared

We also need to eat our daily bread because we are all ministers of reconciliation (2 Cor. 5:11,18 NIV). God chooses to make an appeal to people through us. If we have not eaten our bread (His Word), we won't have the strength nor will we be prepared to give a reason for the hope that we have in Christ (see 1 Pet. 3:15).

I'm always so thankful when the Word of God comes to mind without any conscious thought of my own. There have been many occasions when someone has asked me a question, and I had the answer without fishing for something to say. I recall working with a young lady who came in one morning obviously sad and overwhelmed by her circumstance. We didn't have time to talk, so I asked God for "bread" for her. I wrote the word down, and by afternoon she was able to share her plight. How I rejoiced because her exact and specific answer was on the paper written before she told me her problem. Now some would say that was the gift of the Spirit at work. I don't disagree necessarily, but without His daily bread, I would have had nothing to write. His Word was on my heart, and it was available for her restoration.

When we eat His bread, we are always prepared. To pray according to pattern, we're asking God to equip us with His Word so that no matter what comes up, good or bad, we are completely nourished with His Word, and Holy Spirit can prompt truth. Thus the Word comes out. I liken this process to a computer which can only divulge what has been placed on the hard drive. If nothing was put in, nothing will come out. If we feed on God's Word regularly, His Word will come up; if we feed on religion, clichés, and rhetoric, they will come up; if we feed on the world, then carnality will show up.

When the Shunammite's son died suddenly, she answered every delay and distraction with the words, *"It is well"* (2 Kings 4:23). Naturally, everything was not well. Her son was dead, yet she spoke truth from her heart instead of an obvious fact. It was the truth that sustained her as she wrapped her arms around Elisha's legs, and it was the truth that enabled her to receive back her dead child (see 2 Kings 4:27-37).

Confessing the Word

In addition, when I receive or eat daily bread, I am confessing God's Word over my life daily. The confessed word is just that: saying His Word; repeating His promises; and articulating truth, the Word of God. We don't have to have a problem in order to confess truth. To declare what the Scriptures say is simply the proactive approach to living by faith.

Many times when we pray, we ask God for things that He's already provided. The provision is the Word of God. The Word is not empty. John 6:63 says, *"It is the Spirit who gives life; the flesh profits nothing. The words that I speak to you are spirit, and they are life."* It is therefore my responsibility as a believer to use the living Word, for it is the Word of God that will make the difference.

Too many Christians live defeated lives because negative and dead words have been our confession most of our lives: "Nothing good ever happens to me," "I never win," and "There are no eligible men to marry." These kinds of statements pigeonhole life and leave the nicest Christians struggling to understand why things aren't the way they planned.

Our words are powerful: *"From the fruit of his mouth a man's stomach is filled; with the harvest from his lips he is satisfied. The tongue has the power of life and death, and those who love it will eat its fruit"* (Prov. 18:20-21 NIV). During this part of prayer, our use of the Word of God can make the difference in our lives. What we say *does* matter; we can eat what He's provided by making confessions, and we can trust God to remind us of His Word when trying situations unexpectedly arise.

The Word can set us free from iniquity, strongholds, problems, and difficult circumstances. The Word can deliver health, prosperity, life, freedom, and every heart's desire. When I pray, *"Give me today my daily bread,"* I'm looking for His Word to be my solution. I'm expecting His Word to work all things out for my good. I'm expecting to live fulfilled because I consciously speak His Word into my life. I'm filled because I eat truth each morning, afternoon, and evening, agreeing with what God has said about my life, even if my feelings rebel.

One of the most profound statements I have ever heard was from Bishop I.V. Hilliard. He said, "The will of God is not automatic." This was my epiphany because I lived my whole Christian life thinking God's will *was* automatic, that whatever He wanted to do He would just do. When I heard this teaching, I understood why so many good Christians with good intentions, good morals, and good habits were living defeated. Personally, I didn't want to follow their example, but until this revelation, I was doing just that; I served, gave, loved, smiled, and lived on cruise control. There were no substantive changes in my life because I wasn't eating my daily bread; I wasn't intentionally confessing His Word.

Confessing the Word is not mental assent. Confessing the Word is developing a discipline to sit down and say what God has said concerning your life and surroundings. Don't make the mistake of discounting the power of His Word by ignoring this part of the pattern for prayer.

The Word is powerful. The first chapter of the Book of John famously begins, *"In the beginning was the Word, and the Word was with God, and the Word was God....And the Word became flesh and dwelt among us"* (John 1:1,14). Jesus said of Himself, *"I am the bread of life. He who comes to Me shall never hunger, and he who believes in Me shall never thirst"* (John 6:35). And He prayed for all His disciples: *"Sanctify them through Thy truth; Thy word is truth"* (John 17:17 KJV).

Start today, use the Scriptures listed below and add others that are specific to your desires in life. Say them diligently just as you eat natural food regularly. You won't regret this daily bread.

Father, Thank You for Bread Today

Today I am happy because I have your wisdom and have gained your understanding. I have pleasantness, peace, and the tree of life today (see Prov. 3:13,17-18).

Today, Father, Your Word is perfect and converts my soul. Your testimony makes me wise, and your statutes are right and make my heart rejoice. Your commandments are pure and enlighten my eyes. The fear of You is clean and endures forever in me. Your judgments are true and righteous altogether. Your Word is more desirable than gold. It's sweeter than honey of a honeycomb. By your Word I am warned, and in keeping Your Word I have reward today (see Ps. 19:7-11).

Those who fear You will be glad when they see me, because I have hoped in Your Word (see Ps. 119:74).

I have scattered seed; therefore, I increase today. I am generous; therefore, I am made rich. I water others; therefore, I am watered today (see Prov. 11:24-25).

You are my hiding place today, Lord. Thank You for preserving me from trouble and surrounding me with songs of deliverance (see Ps. 32:7).

The Lord is my sun and shield; the Lord gives me grace and glory; no good thing do You withhold from me today because I walk uprightly before You (see Ps. 84:11).

No grave trouble will overtake me because I'm righteous (see Prov. 12:21).

I live with the fruit of the Spirit in me. I have love, joy, peace, longsuffering, kindness, goodness, faithfulness, gentleness, and self-control (see Gal. 5:22-23).

I have love that suffers long. I am kind. I don't envy. I don't parade myself. I am not provoked by any. I think no evil. I don't rejoice in iniquity. I rejoice in truth. The love of God is in me and never fails (see 1 Cor. 13:4-8).

The peace of God, which passes all understanding, guards my heart and my mind in Christ Jesus today (see Phil. 4:7).

I am clothed with compassion, kindness, humility, gentleness, and patience. By your grace, I can do all things through Christ who strengthens me (see Col. 3:12; Phil. 4:13).

I am faithful; therefore, I abound with blessing (see Prov. 28:20).

I am no longer a slave to sin, but a slave to righteousness....I no longer live, but Christ lives in me. The life I live in the body, I live by faith in the Son of God, who loved me and gave Himself for me (see Rom. 6:18; Gal. 2:20).

For results, I must recognize that all things come from God and He takes care of His children. Moreover, I am His child.

CHAPTER 19

FORGIVE US OUR DEBTS AS WE FORGIVE OUR DEBTORS

Isn't it interesting that life offers plenty of opportunities for offense, yet God tells His children to forgive? Peter said, *"Lord, how many times shall I forgive my brother when he sins against me?"* (Matt. 18:21-22 NIV). The world says once or twice, yet Jesus tells Peter, *"seventy-seven times."* In other words, there is no limit. Forgiveness is the only option every time.

Offenses may come for many reasons—some are heightened by our own sensitivity; some are impossible to overlook. It's important to note, however, that God doesn't categorize offense. He just says to forgive. In addition, God says He will judge and forgive us by how we forgive others.

At first glance this doesn't seem fair. For instance, if a husband commits adultery while a wife is pregnant and his reasoning is completely ludicrous it would seem grossly unfair for God to hold the wife accountable for her inability to forgive, but in fact He does. Of course His grace is sufficient for her, but God doesn't base His Word on what we think is fair or unjust. God holds each of us accountable for our own behavior, even when we can justify how forgiveness isn't deserving. Be clear, the husband will also be accountable for his behavior, but how God deals with Him isn't determined by the wife; it's determined by God.

I think the story of Abigail and Nabal in First Samuel 25:2-25 is a wonderful example of what I mean biblically. David is prepared to avenge himself because of Nabal's inappropriate response to David's request. Abigail hears what has happened and prepares food and gifts then goes out to meet David before he gets to the property. Abigail's actions saved her family and brought favor to her in the eyes of David, but just as she was rewarded, God intervened *"and returned the wickedness of Nabal on his own head"* (see 1 Sam. 25:39). And David saw God judge the situation and proclaimed, *"Blessed be the Lord, who has pleaded the cause of my reproach from the hand of Nabal, and has kept His servant from evil!"* (1 Samuel 25:39).

To make my point clearer, when one of my three children make a decision that warrants punishment, they're not excused because they were provoked by their sibling. No, each child is accountable for his or her individual behavior. And as children of God, we too are accountable for our own behavior.

We stumble when we approach life justifying our actions rather than asking God to help us when we're hurt from our experience.

Living with resentment and offense in our hearts is not a life in Christ, and that is why we are to use this part of the prayer. It's here that we become vulnerable with God to express our pain and express our desire to live life free from the bondage that comes from holding onto offense. If we practically consider, how utterly distraught would we be to hear we're not forgiven by God because we wouldn't forgive Aunt Sweeny for taking momma's recipe? In that moment, the recipe, along with any other offense will mean absolutely nothing in His presence.

Let me give a weightier example. If we have been forgiven for a debt that we could not pay simply because Jesus sacrificed Himself (though He was blameless and faultless) how can God release us when we choose to hold on to matters of this life.

The best way to put forgiveness in perspective is to consider the parable Jesus told in Matthew 18:21-35. Essentially, there is a man who owes the king money. The king has mercy and forgives the man his debt. The forgiveness given to this man is gracious, so it is astonishing to the servant of the king to see the same man who was forgiven of his enormous debt (10,000 talents which is equal to 50 million silver coins) mercilessly require his fellow servant to repay what was owed him—the equivalent of 100 denarii (which is equal to one hundred silver coins). There is a stark and mammoth difference in the debt owed, yet the one who owed the larger amount and who received forgiveness of debt was unable or unwilling to forgive the debt of someone like himself who owed him significantly less.

This is an analogy of our lives when we compare the cost Jesus paid to forgive our sin debt to the debt/offense we refuse to release when personally offended: *"For He made Him who knew no sin to be sin for us, that we might become the righteousness of God in Him"* (2 Cor. 5:21). Consequently, we are just like the wicked servant spoken of in the parable when we choose not to forgive.

In this part of prayer we must consider the price paid for our salvation above the offenses of man. We must also make a decision to forgive even if emotionally we're not ready.

Mark 11:25 says, *"When you stand praying, if you hold anything against anyone, forgive him, so that your Father in heaven may forgive you your sins"* (NIV). This Scripture is not a suggestion, it is a directive. We, therefore, cannot deny forgiveness no matter how offended we have become. Luke 6:37 says, *"forgive, and you will be forgiven"* (NIV). Our reaction determines God's actions. His actions are based on our obedience.

Stephen was a just man who was unjustly accused of blasphemy against Moses and God. The penalty of such actions was death. As they stoned him, Stephen prayed loudly, *"Lord, do not charge them with this sin."* Then he died (see Acts 7:60). Jesus also set an example for us while dying on the cross; His words were, *"Father, forgive them, for they do not know what they do"* (Luke 23:34).

Having been offended, I remember making a conscious decision to forgive. I based it on several truths: One, *"Love covers a multitude of sins"* (1 Pet. 4:8; Prov. 10:12; 17:9-10). Two, I thought about how I would feel if God didn't forgive me. Three, I didn't want my prayers hindered. And four, there was nothing I could do about it. What was done was done. When my spiritual mother, Dr. Bridget Hilliard shared with me her experience with offense, she used Hebrews 9:14. It is perfect because forgiveness may not be complete with an inner resolve or decision, but the blood of Jesus Christ is sufficient enough to rid hurt, purge resentment, and cleanse the soul. I encourage you to add Hebrews to your confessions listed at the end of the previous chapter and see your *conscience cleansed from dead works so you can serve the Living God* (see Heb. 9:14 NIV). I made a decision to forgive, but I was made free because of the blood of Jesus Christ. You can be free through that blood too.

The motivation to forgive is love. The love you receive as a child of God, as well as the love we are constrained to show according to First Corinthians 13:4-7, is the reason we must let go of offense.

The key to praying this part of the pattern is to recognize our fallibility and set our eyes on the finished work of Christ. We must be as honest as possible with God, sharing the state of our heart, revealing our shortcomings, and admitting to any personal role that led to the offense. For some there may have been no role at all. For others, the role may have been so miniscule it's been easy to dismiss it and place the blame elsewhere. Then there are some of us who played a large part in the offense that eventually became our own. In any case, God is able to hear the cry of our heart if we'll give the situation to Him, choosing His ways and not our own (see Prov. 16:25; Isa. 55:8-9). In our obedience to forgive and release offense, we will see a table set before us in the presence of our enemies (see Ps. 23:5). Our God will be our vindication (see Ps. 24:5), and He will honor His promise to avenge and repay (see Rom. 12:19) where necessary.

Forgiveness isn't easy, but it is necessary for our own well-being (spiritual, emotional, and mental). Our intention should be to forgive, and by faith even to forget the sin. In other words, the offense should no longer be available for perfect recall but should be washed away by the blood of Christ.

When we realize how hard forgiveness is, it becomes necessary for an earnest and sincere cry to God regarding the state of our own heart. Look at this key passage from Psalm 51 with me:

> *Have mercy upon me, O God, according to Your loving kindness; according to the multitude of Your tender mercies, blot out my transgressions. Wash me thoroughly from my iniquity, and cleanse me from my sin. For I acknowledge my transgressions, and my sin is*

always before me....Purge me with hyssop, and I shall be clean; wash me, and I shall be whiter than snow. Make me hear joy and gladness....Create in me a clean heart, O God, and renew a steadfast spirit within me. Do not cast me away from Your presence, and do not take Your Holy Spirit from me. Restore the joy of Your salvation and uphold me by your generous Spirit (Psalm 51:1-3,7;10-12).

After we pray, trusting in His infallibility, then we must eat daily bread (see Chapter 6) regarding forgiveness. We confess His truth until our heart changes. Don't let the enemy trick you into thinking that time heals wounds and your heart may eventually change. That is a risk I encourage you to avoid. Pursue inward peace and free yourself. You cannot change the Word of God, but the Word of God can change you.

Father,
I need You to heal my heart so I can forgive and walk in love. I desire to release those who have offended me (see Matt. 18:21-23). I desire to show my love for You through my obedience (see John 14:23), so I yield what I don't honestly understand completely. Wash me from everything that would hinder a sincere relationship with You. I choose You and Your ways.
I repent for holding a grudge and keeping resentment and anger. These are not your characteristics (see Gal. 5:22-23). I choose to allow the blood of Jesus Christ to cleanse my conscience from dead works so that I may serve You (see Heb. 9:13-14). I put on the Lord Jesus Christ (see Rom. 13:14).

May my love abound more and more in knowledge
and depth of insight so that I may approve the
things that are excellent, that I may be sincere and
without offense until the day of Christ (see
Phil. 1:9-10).
I forgive by faith in Christ Jesus. I love by faith in
Christ Jesus. I'm free by the power of the blood
shed by Christ Jesus.
Thank You, Lord, in Jesus' name. Amen.

For results in praying the pattern, we must be honest with ourselves. There must be a willingness to humble ourselves and forgive. Release people for the wrong done to us.

CHAPTER 20

AND DO NOT LEAD US INTO TEMPTATION

Let me begin this chapter by making sure I am clear on this point: God does not tempt man. James 1:13 says, *"Let no one say when he is tempted, 'I am tempted by God', for God cannot be tempted by evil, nor does He Himself tempt anyone. But each one is tempted when he is drawn away by his own desires and enticed. Then when desire has conceived, it gives birth to sin; and sin, when it is full-grown, brings forth death."* So, let it be said outright, God tempts no one.

Temptation is anything that takes the believer away from truth. Temptation is far beyond lust for a man or woman, far beyond desire for a piece of cake. The ultimate temptation is to cause believers to doubt God and throw away their confidence in Him. Temptation comes to stunt the growth of a baby Christian and destroy the faith of a lifetime believer. Temptation causes a person to second-guess the love of God, the presence of God, the will of God, and the power of God. Temptation is designed to talk the believer out of truth into distorted realities. Is it any wonder that we need to pray, "Lord, lead me not into temptation"? The difficulty for most of us is understanding why Jesus used the word *lead* in the first place; why did He phrase the prayer in this way? Let me digress a bit in order to help us pray this portion effectively.

Temptation always counters the Word of God, so when we believe feelings, trust reasoning, give credibility to facts, or question the validity of God's Word, we are in effect giving place to temptation. It is logic at work for the world, but sin to you and me as Christians.

Jesus said in John 17:15-17, *"I do not pray that You should take them out of the world, but that You should keep them from the evil one. They are not of the world, just as I am not of the world. Sanctify them by Your truth. Your word is truth."*

Jesus prayed for His disciples regarding the influence of satan and the world. He did not ask God to anoint them, or to make them powerful or great; He prayed that they would be protected from the system of the world and the plot and plans of the enemy. Specifically He said, *"keep them from the evil one…sanctify them by Your truth."*

We face the same system and the same devil. This means we must pray when situations in life oppose what God has promised. Victory over temptation requires more than sheer determination.

When I was prepared to walk away from church and God because of offense, I was being tempted. My decision to continue in the faith during this time of inner turmoil and pain came after I sought God and He reminded me of truth: God isn't who He is because of humankind's carelessness or the church's failings. God is not true because of my financial affairs, good or bad. God is God, plain and simple. Who I am, what I have, what I think, and what I experience has no bearing on who He is and what He has promised. Second Timothy 2:11-14 says it best: *"If we died with Him, we shall also live with Him. If we endure, we shall also reign with Him. If we deny Him, He also will deny us. If we are faithless, He remains faithful; He cannot deny Himself."* To turn my back on Him would be to yield to temptation and prove my salvation was not based on faith in Christ but on my emotional state.

While in the Garden of Gethsemane, Jesus says to His disciples, *"Watch and pray, lest you enter into temptation. The spirit indeed is willing, but the flesh is weak"* (Matt. 26:41). In other words, "I know you mean well, but you need to pray if you expect to remain in Me (the Word)." They fell asleep and shortly thereafter, gave way to temptation and were scattered (see Matt. 26:31; Mark 14:27).

Luke 22:31-32 records Jesus' conversation with Peter. He tells him, *"Simon, Simon, Satan has asked to sift you as wheat. But I have prayed for you, Simon, that your faith may not fail"* (NIV). I'll say it again, God does not tempt! He doesn't want us scattered, or our faith to fail. God doesn't want His children to be unbelieving but believing. God has no desire to see His children lost. If that were so, we didn't need Jesus; we were already lost. The answer for temptation is prayer. Never ignore the prompting of God to pray. It could make the difference between remaining in Christ or walking away from truth.

Tests: God's Heart Gauge

Now note, *God does test us.* Testing may seem troubling, but it has value. Imagine school without any testing. How would you qualify for promotion? There would be no comprehensive way to know your state, there would be no challenge, and there would be no closure.

God doesn't mind giving tests. He tested Israel as they traveled the desert placing various obstacles in front of them to see their response (see Exod. 15:26;16:4) God tested the people going to war with Gideon to ensure the right men went to war (see Judges 7:4). God withdrew from Hezekiah in order to know what was in his heart (see 2 Chron. 32:31). And lest we feel absolved from the test, God tells us in James 1:1 that our faith will be tested.

A test enables Him to see sincerity and truth from the heart of those who say they love Him. He looks for people who prove—not just state—but prove their love when circumstances overshadow what they have professed and make it look like He is not true to His Word.

And so God uses the devil, who brings temptation, for the test. Isaiah 54:15-16 says, *"If anyone does attack you, it will not be my doing; whoever attacks you will surrender to you. 'See, it is I who created the blacksmith who fans the coals into flame and forges a weapon fit for its work. And it is I who have created the destroyer to work havoc'"* (NIV). God makes a purpose for the devil, but He also tells us as believers the end result in verse 17: *"'No weapon forged against you will prevail, and you will refute every tongue that accuses you. This is the heritage of the servants of the Lord, and this is their vindication from Me,' declares the Lord."*

The devil tempts you so he can bring accusations against you in the presence of God, but Revelation 12:10-11 reveals truth: *"Then I heard a loud voice saying in heaven, 'Now salvation, and strength, and the kingdom of our God, and the power of His Christ have come,* ***for the accuser of our brethren, who accused them before our God day and night, has been cast down.*** *And they overcame him by the* *blood of the Lamb and by the word of their testimony, and they did not love their lives to the death.'"*

The blood has been shed; now what comes out of your mouth is up to you. Do you really believe what you profess? Do you really love God? If everything went awry in life, would you still love and serve God? These are the basic questions that you will answer during the test. Not in theory, but in reality.

When temptations are present, the state of the heart is being tested. Jeremiah 17:5-8 talks about a curse on those whose heart departs from God and a blessing on those who trust and hope in the Lord. To depart from God is very simple. It doesn't have to look like complete apostasy, but can be ever so slight. We still go to church; we still sing and serve, but our expectation is different, and our trust is misplaced. It's when we no longer believe God's Word but give greater credence to another while holding a pious demeanor.

God gauges our hearts during a test. And like any test, there is a price for failing and promotion for passing. You can pass your test as you pray the way Jesus taught.

God's intention is to find someone whose heart is loyal to Him: *"For the eyes of the Lord run to and fro throughout the whole earth, to show Himself strong on behalf of those whose heart is loyal to Him"* (2 Chron. 16:9). As such, it's in the test (i.e., hardship, wilderness, storm, trial, or desert) that the temptation can be found and our loyalty ascertained. Loyalty speaks to allegiance good, bad, or ugly. Loyalty is not swayed by circumstances or feelings. Loyalty is constant.

Job was loyal. The Bible says he was a righteous man, and he was tested. Everything he had was taken away from him. It looks like Job did something wrong, but if we look closely, it wasn't what Job did wrong that brought the hardship; it was what he did right: *"Then the Lord said to Satan, 'Have you considered My servant Job, that there is none like him on the earth, a blameless and upright man, one who fears God and shuns evil?'"* (Job 1:8). Satan, the accuser, answered God, *"Does Job fear God for nothing? Have You not made a hedge around him, around his household, and around all that he has on every side? You have blessed the work of his hands, and his possessions have increased in the land. But stretch out Your hand and touch all that he has, and he will surely curse You to Your face!"* (Job 1:9-11). Satan's goal was to push Job to curse God. He has the same goal in your life; he wants to push you over the edge so you change, curse, or concede.

All of the promises of God are received by faith, and when you are in a faith fight it is the devil's plan to get you to sabotage what you're believing God to do in your life by getting you to speak words of doubt and unbelief. If you can continue saying the promise, if you can remain in His Word, then His Word will come to pass. If you capitulate, you will never see the promise fulfilled and you'll always see the promises of God as theory only.

I met a woman who was really going through a hard time with her ex-husband. He wasn't kind toward her and was quite devious as courts swayed in his favor. She responded to him according to the Bible and in the end lost every material thing. She felt cheated and robbed and from the looks of it, she was. My consolation to her wasn't that she lost but that she was still in her faith fight. Continue confessing God's promise, continue speaking life to a dead situation. Not because you're unbalanced but because you trust God and you're convinced there is absolutely nothing too hard for Him and nothing out of His reach. If His Word says it, then it's a possibility to those who believe. Just because the courts said it was over didn't mean anything. Sadly, she became distracted, believed the lie, and could no longer remain in His Word. That situation was a test of her heart. God had not left her, though she felt betrayed. God had not brought shame to her, but the devil convinced her to concede, curse God, and move on with life. She yielded to the temptation to quit God, and to this day (to my knowledge), she has not stepped into the house of God. She failed that test. You see, God expects us to remain faithful to the promise and faithful to Him even when we're under attack. It's our faith that's being tested. What we believe in our heart will be revealed when we're under fire. I'm not saying the test isn't hard and the fire hot, but I am saying there is more going on around you than what is apparent to the natural eye.

We're like Job in those testing times, completely oblivious to the heavenly conversation. For Job, he lost his children, his wealth, and his reputation. He could have yielded to the temptation to curse God because of his plight. He could have yielded to the temptation to base God's righteousness and relevance on his blessed status, but even in pain and hurt, we learn that *"Job did not sin nor charge God with wrong"* (Job 1:22). Job passed the test, and God tells satan, *"And still he holds fast to his integrity"* (Job 2:3). Satan decides the attack wasn't strong enough and reasons that if he strikes his flesh Job will waver. However, *"in all this Job did not sin with his lips"* (Job 2:10). In other words, he did not give in to the temptation.

Jesus became an example of testing, too. Matthew 4:1-11 records the account of Jesus' temptation in the wilderness: *"Jesus was led up by the Spirit into the wilderness to be tempted by the devil"* (Matt. 4:1). Notice that it was the Spirit who led Jesus into the wilderness.

Could it be that some of the situations we experience in life are by the leading of the Holy Spirit? Jesus took the test and remained loyal to His calling and purpose regardless of the temptations satan presented. He passed by saying, "It is written"—by countering satan's challenges with truth.

First Corinthians 10:13 reads, *"No temptation has overtaken you except such as is common to man; but God is faithful, who will not allow you to be tempted beyond what you are able, but with the temptation will also make the way of escape, that you may be able to bear it."*

Based on pattern, our words are not simply to mimic, *"Lead me not into temptation,"* but to cry to God for a heart that is so loyal to Him that truth remains. It is a prayer to Holy Spirit to remind us of God's Word in spite of our difficulty, pain, and heartache. We're not just asking God to lead us not into temptation; we're asking Him to so fill us with Himself that our hearts always choose the way of escape, Jesus Christ. Like Jesus, we're asking that the cup pass from us, but we're before His presence for the strength to drink it anyway if it is His will (see Matt. 26:39,42). When life contradicts the Word of God, we're praying that we pass the test because our heart is committed to truth, integrity, righteousness, and humility.

Every Christian will be tested. First Corinthians 10:12-13 says, *"So, if you think you are standing firm, be careful that you don't fall! No temptation has seized you except what is common to man"* (NIV). We will all prove who we are and what we really believe. If we'll follow the example of Jesus during His wilderness experience, I believe the test will end sooner than later. Jesus' test didn't last long because He used the Word immediately. When we wallow in sorrow, anger, pity, or denial during the test, the temptations linger. When we abide in truth, the temptation loses its grip, the test ends, and we are victorious.

If God allows the devil to tempt you, will He be disappointed because you gave in to the temptation to deny Him? Or will you be proven sincere in your love for God? *"...and the rain descended, the floods came and the winds blew and beat on that house; and it did not fall, for it was founded on the rock"* (Matt. 7:25) Pray that your house is built on the foundation that keeps you standing in the end.

[Remember, trials] *"come so that your faith*—*of greater worth than gold, which perishes even though refined by fire*—**may be proved genuine and may result in praise, glory and honor when Jesus Christ is revealed"** (1 Pet. 1:7 NIV).

Pray.

> *Father,*
> *Cleanse me from secret faults, and keep me back*
> *from presumptuous sins; let them not have*
> *dominion over me. Then I shall be blameless and*
> *innocent of great transgression. May the words of*
> *my mouth and the meditation of my heart be*
> *acceptable in Your sight, O Lord, my strength and*
> *my Redeemer (see Ps. 19:12-14).*
> *Lord, may my heart be steadfast toward You,*
> *acknowledging You in all my ways. Save me, Lord,*
> *and I shall be saved. Heal me, and I shall be*
> *healed (see Jer. 17:14). In the tests of life may I*
> *never turn to test You by questioning Your ability*
> *(see Ps. 78:17-20) by asking "Can you?", but with*
> *confidence may I stand in the midst of every*
> *situation and declare,*
> *"Lord, You are my hiding place, and You preserve*
> *me with songs of deliverance" (see Ps. 32:7).*
> *Purify my heart, O God, that I may see You (see*
> *Matt. 5:8).*
> *In Jesus' Name. Amen.*

For results in praying "lead me not into temptation," we must recognize that God does not tempt. He does test us, and to pass the test we must make an earnest plea for a clean heart. Then temptations will have no foothold.

CHAPTER 21

BUT DELIVER US FROM THE EVIL ONE

This part of the prayer really is a continuation of *"lead us not into temptation."* When we recognize it is the devil who tempts and then condemns, we must appreciate the saving power of Jehovah. Our prayer is founded upon a trust that God delivers us from every unforeseen scenario in life.

If you can envision a parent redirecting an inquisitive toddler away from danger, you have a good idea of how deliverance works in this prayer. *Deliver* in the Greek means, "rescue." So we can say, "Lord, rescue me away from the evil one. When I don't know any better, redirect me." Just as a toddler has to be "run away" from the edge of a lake so that she can play safely within the confines of the playground, we also need the intervention of God in our lives. When we find ourselves inadvertently standing in front of the adversary, this "run us away" is our cry for help from God.

Second Peter 2:9 talks about God's willingness to deliver or rescue *"the godly out of temptations and to reserve the unjust under punishment for the day of judgment, and especially those who walk according to the flesh in the lust of uncleanness and despise authority."* Noah and Lot are two examples of men delivered from evil. Both were in an ungodly place upholding righteousness. The enemy would love for it to look like God throws the baby out with the bath water, but we can see God's willingness not only to separate the godly from the evil, but to deliver them completely.

First Corinthians 10:13 states that *"God is faithful."* The faithfulness of God enables us to believe that He will always *"make the way of escape"* from temptations to live like the world or succumb to the flesh (1 Cor. 10:13). This escape is also being supernaturally removed from dire straights.

When Daniel and the Hebrew boys were in Babylonian captivity, they were faced with the temptation not only to eat like the other people ate, but to conform to idolatry. The Book of Daniel tells of many opportunities these young men had to faint, to doubt God, to give up, and to surrender to the plan of the enemy, but they chose to live a righteous course. Each time the test came, they called on God, and each time God delivered them.

Whether it was choosing not to bow before the golden image (though everyone else did), or choosing not to eat the king's delicacies, or choosing not to pray to Nebuchadnezzar's god, these men made a conscious decision to please God. Their commitment to God enabled them to resist temptation and remain in truth. As a result, they saw God deliver them with great power from the hand of the evil one every time. From the death sentence of Nebuchadnez-zar, to the fiery furnace, to the lion's den, God's faithfulness rescued them from the plans of the evil one.

Even today, Christians are put in situations that mock standards of righteousness. The confrontation can be ominous, but if we'll hold our course, God will deliver us from the temptation to compromise or give up. He will deliver us—rescue us—from the evil one. Recently my husband gave a prophetic word to a brother about upholding a righteous stand in his job. He told him it would get hard, but in the end it would be the best decision he made. Not even two weeks later, the brother came back to report how he did as Pastor said, and while the majority of his floor was laid off, the job kept him. Glory to God! He was delivered from the evil one's attempt to add him to the thousands who have unexpectedly lost their jobs.

The enemy presents temptations that make us want to doubt God, second-guess truth, or follow logic instead of faith. As we remain faithful to God, we'll see our lives delivered from the evil one: *"From the Lord comes deliverance. May Your blessing be on Your people"* (Ps. 3:8 NIV).

When Job and Jesus were tempted, they talked to God, declared truth, and came out of their test with hearts that were proven. The same is true for us according to James 1:12, *"Blessed is the man who endures temptation; for when he has been approved, he will receive the crown of life which the Lord has promised to those who love Him."* How wonderful to know that the temptation we endure proves our love and devotion to God. Thus the enemy must flee (see James 4:7).

Our prayer to be delivered from the evil one is also a request for strength, stamina, and fortitude to uphold righteousness and obedience without intimidation from the enemy. Like Moses who *"refused to be known as the son of Pharaoh's daughter. He chose to be mistreated along with the people of God rather than to enjoy the pleasures of sin for a short time. He regarded disgrace for the sake of Christ as of greater value than the treasures of Egypt, because he was looking ahead to his reward. By faith he left Egypt, not fearing the king's anger; he persevered because he saw Him who is invisible"* (Heb. 11:24-27 NIV). Just like Moses, you can be delivered from accusation, threat, and upheaval by yielding to God and trusting that He sees and will step in to intervene.

Our church purchased land almost five years ago. It was a triumphant day as we signed papers and began clearing trees, obtaining permits, setting dates for occupancy. We were so happy because this would enable our people to move from a school into our own building. The people were delighted and so were we. Then everything came to a halt as the market turned upside down and the bank, (then the banks) that committed to us began reneging on the deal. The enemy was blocking us and trying to discourage us, but we continued in faith, we continued praying with thanksgiving, we continued confessing, "Our building is finished, filled and free of debt" and just like the God of old, He didn't just deliver us, He honored us. One day we owned empty acres of land and the next day we had another piece of property, buildings, and extra revenue from an existing business on the property! So while we were hindered from building on the original piece of land, that didn't stop God. We'll be in a position to heed His will by moving out of the school into our own before years end. On top of that, we still own the other property and plans continue. I tell you, God can always deliver; it just rarely comes the way you expect it!

Ephesians 6:10-18 says,

Finally, be strong in the Lord and in His mighty power. Put on the full armor of God so that you can take your stand against the devil's schemes.

*For our struggle is not against flesh and blood,
but against the rulers, against the authorities,
against the powers of this dark world and against
the spiritual forces of evil in the heavenly realms.
Therefore put on the full armor of God, so that
when the day of evil comes, you may be able to
stand your ground, and after you have done
everything, to stand. **Stand firm then, with the
belt of truth** buckled around your waist, **with** the
breastplate of **righteousness** in place, and with
your feet fitted **with the readiness that comes from
the gospel of peace.** In addition to all this, take up
the **shield of faith,** with which you can extinguish
all the flaming arrows of the evil one. Take **the
helmet of salvation** and **the sword of the Spirit,
which is the word of God. And pray** in the Spirit
on all occasions **with all kind of prayers and**
requests. With this in mind, **be alert** and always
keep on **praying for all** the saints" (NIV).*

See the Lord's Prayer as a pattern. To be delivered from the evil one is to be strong in the Lord. I can pray those words rote, or I can take responsibility and put on the armor of God. If I wear the armor, then I'll be strong enough to resist the temptation to compromise truth. I'll also be alert enough to pray for others.

Peter took off his belt of truth when he saw how they treated Jesus. Peter removed the breastplate of righteousness when he stopped walking with the Lord and the other disciples. Peter, because he was afraid, took off his shoes that would point people to Christ. Peter fainted in faith and dropped his shield. Peter laid his sword (the Words of Christ) down. Peter denied the Christ and took off his helmet of salvation.

Yet God is faithful! And when Jesus came to visit the disciples before going to be glorified, He called for Peter and asked Him, *"Simon son of John, do you truly love me?"* (John 21:16 NIV). Peter replied yes and became a voice for generations to hear and read about. Peter was restored so he could go and strengthen his brothers.

God can deliver you too. When we ask our Father to deliver us from the evil one, we must understand that He will! The evil one is any antagonistic, anti-Christ spirit that has come your way. Paul said, *"And the Lord will deliver me from every evil work and preserve me for His heavenly kingdom. To Him be glory forever and ever. Amen!"* (2 Tim. 4:18).

Now, woman of God, man of God, put on your armor and hold your ground. First Peter 5:8-10 says, *"Be self-controlled and alert. Your enemy the devil prowls around like a roaring lion looking for someone to devour. Resist him, standing firm in the faith, because you know that your brothers throughout the world are undergoing the same kind of sufferings. And the God of all grace, who called you to His eternal glory in Christ, after you have suffered a little while, will Himself restore you and make you strong, firm and steadfast. To Him be the power for ever and ever. Amen"* (NIV).

> *Thank You, Father, for being my shield* (see Ps. 33:20) *and my defense. I praise You for Your promise to preserve me from all evil and to preserve my soul* (see Ps. 121:7). *You are my help, and I look to You to show Yourself strong in my life. You provide a way of escape for me in every temptation I face because You are faithful* (see 1 Cor. 10:13). *You said when the enemy comes like a flood that You would raise a standard against him* (see Isa. 59:19). *You also told me that I have been*

redeemed, so I choose not to fear. Though I pass through the waters or rivers they will not overflow me because You are with me. You said if I walk through the fire I shall not be burned, neither shall the flame scorch me (see Isa. 43:1-3). All because You are the Lord my God!
I take confidence in You (see Prov. 3:26). Thank You for delivering my life from destruction (see Ps. 103:4), and giving me victory in this life. I trust You to deliver me from every plot and plan of the enemy. May my life be pleasing to You and my heart be completely loyal to You, just because of who You are:
My Father, My Friend, My God.
I praise and thank You, Lord. In Christ's Name.
Amen.

For results in praying, have confidence in the faithfulness of God in your life.

He will never leave you defenseless.

CHAPTER 22

FOR YOURS IS THE KINGDOM AND THE POWER AND THE GLORY FOREVER. AMEN.

The last part of the Lord's Prayer is what we normally hear at the beginning of most people's prayers. Yet, Jesus teaches us to acknowledge His sovereignty, power, and authority at the end of the Lord's Prayer. If we'll appreciate the pattern of prayer, we won't just say these final words alone; we'll use these words to guide us in adoration and praise of our God who has been so faithful to us.

At this point in our fellowship with our Father we recognize Him as God. He's not just one of the gods; He is the true and living God! We should consider who it is we serve at this point; there is nothing He cannot do, and there is no situation of which He is unaware. Though He's invisible, He is all-seeing, all-knowing and all-powerful. When we pray now, it's with reflection, homage, joy, and a decision to applaud His greatness.

Because of His greatness, we must praise Him! *"Great is the Lord, and greatly to be praised; and His greatness is unsearchable"* (Ps. 145:3). He is the Creator of all things, and it's by His will that we are created and have our being (see Rev. 4:11). During this part of the prayer, we also express our thanks for His kindness and for every answered prayer. Now is the time to exalt the Lord with abandoned hearts.

One of the mistakes made at this point in prayer is to rely upon feelings. It's very easy to skip this time to acknowledge God because we simply don't feel like it. Rain, lack of sleep, bankruptcy, illness, any range of things in life can prove to be a deterrent to praise. Yet this is our responsibility as the righteous. Psalm 33:1 says, *"Sing joyfully to the Lord, you righteous; it is fitting for the upright to praise Him"* (NIV). Psalm 150:6 says, *"Let everything that has breath praise the Lord"* (NIV). Isaiah 61:3 tells us that Jesus was anointed to bestow on us *"the oil of joy for mourning, the garment of praise for the spirit of heaviness."* Too often, we assume we praise and exalt God when we feel good, but that is not the case. We are to praise God, period. Our praise is not circumstantial or based on custom; our praise is continuous and based on covenant. It's for His glory, and though there is benefit to the one who praises, it really is about acknowledgment and declaration. We acknowledge His greatness now and forever, and we declare His Kingdom, power, and glory without end.

One of the best times to praise is when you don't feel good, when you may be uncertain and fearful. When you praise anyway, you confuse the devil and truly honor God. When you praise God during times of hardship, you are magnifying God above the situations that you face. When you declare through praise His sufficiency to handle anything and everything, our God comes to show Himself in your life in ways never imagined.

I remember being single and asking the Lord what age I would be when I married. Little did I know at the time that some were saying I would be an old spinster. But God told me how old I would be and from His report I was quite content. And then, I was a year before that age with no prospects and no interests. I had two options. I could panic and begin sulking about how I hadn't met anyone and how I work so much that no one would find me if they tried. I could have counted my hearing from God defective and cancelled His promise based on my words of doubt, but I chose my second option, which was to continue giving glory to God. I want this to help you if you're single and believing God. I didn't continue at my same level of commitment to God; I gave more. I figured the devil would step aside if I start growing stronger in Christ and I start doing more for the Kingdom. If I praise, God will be pleased, and the devil will get out of the way just to shut me up. It worked. I made my singlehood count through my praise and dedication and let me tell you, I was married at the age God promised! And I'll celebrate fifteen years in August 2009. That's the power of God at work when we praise Him instead of complain, grumble, and focus on the problem. Nothing is too hard for Him!

We worship by acknowledging His ability, but our praise comes by thanking Him for who He is in greatness. To praise God is to applaud His magnificent works. To praise is to shout with triumph and celebrate His response to our cry (whether we see our answer or not). This time of adulation should happen even if answers are unseen. That's what faith is all about: *"...the substance of things hoped for, the evidence of things not seen"* (Heb. 11:1 KJV). Joshua is a wonderful example of that. He led Israel to praise God after marching around the walls of Jericho. With the shout to God the walls came down and victory belonged to Israel (Joshua 6).

Our culture has taught us from the time we were children to thank a person *after* a gesture is made or a gift is given, but with God, we should give thanks and praise *before* we actually see any change or difference. That's what Jehoshaphat and Joshua did. We shouldn't wait to say thank you or acknowledge His hand in our lives. We should be proactive and show the same level of intense joy and thanksgiving *before we see* the results of our prayer *as we do after we see* the results of prayer.

In our family there are times when we have what we call a "Praise Break." We have no rules or schedule for how we praise. Regardless of how things are going (our way or not), we'll stop our routine just to praise and thank God for His goodness, for His kindness, and for answered prayer. We shout with thanksgiving and jump for joy. We celebrate Him and His blessings. We're pleasing God and making what we have by faith become our reality a little sooner.

Moreover, to praise God is a wonderful way to conclude fellowship with Him.

The Lord's Prayer can be our genuine expression of love, adoration, and trust in our Father and God. If we consider this prayer beyond words alone and apply with intention and sincerity the pattern Jesus taught, we are sure to find needs met and fulfillment in every aspect of our lives.

The Lord's Prayer is a pattern that can change our lives if we'll begin to do what Jesus taught.

May our God , show Himself faithful in your life as you pursue Him in this pattern of prayer. As it is written, *"Draw near to God and He will draw near to you"* (James 4:8).

For Yours Is the Kingdom and the Power and the Glory Forever Amen.

You are the all-powerful, omnipotent God.
You are the omniscient, all-knowing God. You are
an omnipresent God. You are everywhere, and in
You I have fullness of joy. You are great and
marvelous are Your works. Just and true are all of
Your ways, O King of the saints. Who shall not
fear You and glorify Your name? For all the
nations will bow in reverence of Your name (see
Rev. 15:3-4).
You are beautiful and altogether lovely. You are
God, and there is no one who compares to You. Be
glorified in Heaven and earth. Let everything that
has breath praise Your name forever (see
Ps. 150:6).

To follow the pattern of prayer, in conclusion, is to know
who you are and to whom you belong. When you understand
these things, your praise will be without limits, and He will
come to inhabit you.

PRAYER OF SALVATION

If you don't know Jesus Christ as your personal Lord and Savior, you can know Him today. Simply pray the following prayer from your heart and begin your fellowship with Him as Jesus taught. Your life will never be the same.

> *Father, you said if I confess with my mouth the Lord Jesus and believe in my heart that God has raised Him from the dead, I will be saved* (see Rom. 10:9 NIV).

> *Father, I confess Jesus Christ as Your Son who came to take away the sins of the world. I believe unto righteousness and confess unto salvation* (see Rom. 10:10 NIV).

> *I repent for my sins and ask You to come into my life today* (see Matt. 3:2 NIV). *Thank you Father.*

> *From this day onward, may my life represent You and may You be pleased with what I say, what I do, where I go, and who I am. I belong to You.* (see Matt. 3:8 NIV).

> *Thank You, Father, for receiving me* (John 6:37).

D. Qwynn Gross is co-founder and Executive Pastor of Hope Cathedral in Jackson, NJ. Ordained as an Elder in 2005, Elder Qwynn is known as a powerful intercessor and practical teacher of the Gospel. Her passion is to stir the hearts of people toward a greater commitment to God. Elder Qwynn and her husband, Pastor Trevón, have three children: Trevón, Jr., Dianna, and Sarah Gross.

D. Qwynn Gross is available for workshops, seminars, and speaking engagements.

REQUESTS SHOULD BE SENT TO:

Steadfast Hope Ministries
460 W. Veterans Highway
Jackson, NJ 08527

Phone: 732-928-9072
www.steadfasthope.org

Additional copies of this book and other
book titles from DESTINY IMAGE are
available at your local bookstore.

Call toll-free: 1-800-722-6774.

Send a request for a catalog to:

Destiny Image® Publishers, Inc.

P.O. Box 310
Shippensburg, PA 17257-0310

*"Speaking to the Purposes of God for This
Generation and for the Generations to Come."*

**For a complete list of our titles,
visit us at www.destinyimage.com.**